The Mystery and the Passion

The Mystery and the Passion

Richard Hasnip

Authentic

MILTON KEYNES ● COLORADO SPRINGS ● HYDERABAD

Copyright © 2009 Richard Hasnip

15 14 13 12 11 10 09   7 6 5 4 3 2 1

First published 2009 by Authentic Media
9 Holdom Avenue, Bletchley, Milton Keynes,
Bucks, MK1 1QR, UK
1820 Jet Stream Drive, Colorado Springs, CO 80921, USA
OM Authentic Media, Medchal Road, Jeedimetla Village,
Secunderabad 500 055, A.P., India
www.authenticmedia.co.uk
Authentic Media is a division of IBS-STL U.K., limited by
guarantee, with its Registered Office at Kingstown Broadway,
Carlisle, Cumbria CA3 0HA.
Registered in England & Wales No. 1216232.
Registered charity 270162

The right of Richard Hasnip to be identified as the Author of this
Work has been asserted by him in accordance with the
Copyright, Designs and Patents Act 1988.

British Library Cataloguing in Publication Data

A catalogue record for this book is available from the
British Library

ISBN-13: 978-1-85078-827-0

Cover Design by MOOSE77
Print Management by Adare
Printed and bound in Great Britain by
J.F. Print, Sparkford

Contents

Introduction

They say the world is changing. They say we live in post-modern times.

As a society, we have lost our faith in evidence.

Scientists can tell us incredible things about how we got here – but they can't make us care. And the truth is – no one really cares about *how* we came to be, not any more. The contemporary debate has moved on. Instead we want to know how to live now we *are* here. We want to know *why* we're here. And for those answers science is as helpless as it's always been.

So people go to the same place they've always gone: they go back to stories.

The theatre is a house built to tell stories, but the stories it is telling no longer answer the needs of the people, and the people have started to notice.

The church has answers. It has a book full of stories, some of the most important stories ever told. But the church has forgotten how to tell them, and that has been noticed too.

The church and the theatre need each other. The theatre needs the stories that tell people how and why to live. It needs to mean something again. And the church needs the ways and means to get those stories heard.

This book is divided into two parts. In the first part I look at the theatre and the church: their shared history, their current relationship and where they might be going. In the second, I've included two plays that can be performed by churches or drama groups in which some of the ideas discussed can be put into practice.

Both of the plays have been tested in performance and I have found them useful and effective. I trust you will too. The important thing, though, is not that lots of people perform my plays. The important thing is that the church and the theatre rediscover one another.

I've written this book because I can see a future where people share life-changing stories and God-breathed Scripture like they *mean it*, where congregations and audiences laugh and cry, experiencing and sharing what it is to be human as well as experiencing and worshipping God.

If you try it, you might love it. If you love it, you'll work hard at it. If you work hard at it you could become very good at it – and then who knows what might be possible?

It just needs people to try it.

If you think you might be one of those people – read on, and welcome.

One

Like Father, Like Son

Anyone who loves theatre knows how exciting it can be. They know about the spine-tingling moments that can take place; how the air is charged; how an audience of total strangers can be brought together through shared emotion, tears or laughter. Theatre can make us experience powerful unseen forces and leave us shaken and changed. It can provoke debate and powerful feelings, but it can also affirm beliefs and reinforce a tradition, a culture or shared values. In short, theatre can be great.

There have been two massive influences on the direction my life has taken. One is my Christian faith; a faith that I learned from my parents and gradually discovered for myself as I was growing up.

The other is the theatre. I suppose this came gradually too. I had a brilliant drama teacher at school called John Butcher (Mr Butcher to me, at the time) who made the subject enormous fun, but also important and worthy of serious study. But there was also a night at the theatre that probably sealed my fate. I went to London to see the Royal Shakespeare Company's production of King Lear with Robert Stephens in the title role.

The late, great Robert Stephens was a truly awesome actor who was capable of being monumental as well as profoundly real. He gave a virtuoso performance that night: one that combined enormous power with a surprising tenderness. But I suspect it was the play that affected me on that occasion as much as the lead actor. It was exciting and moving, and it seemed to ask fundamental questions of us in the audience as well as of God.

By the time the night ended I was on my feet applauding with tears in my eyes. Reading this you might assume that I'm a typical 'luvvie' given to gushing sentimentality. I can assure you that is not the case. Generally speaking (unless I'm acting) I'm uncomfortable with extravagant displays of emotion. But the performance of that play got to me that night. If you don't like theatre then you won't know what I'm talking about. But if you do, then I think (and hope) that you will have had an experience like that at some point in your life. I think it's why you and I keep going back – we're looking for that experience again.

But sadly, anyone who loves theatre (at least in the UK) knows that this doesn't happen very often. It seems that the most common emotion experienced by theatre lovers today is boredom. We have talented actors, clever playwrights and inventive directors but somehow the excitement seems to have gone out of the whole affair. The spirit is willing but the flesh is weak, or perhaps the flesh is willing and the spirit is . . . strangely absent. In his foreword for *To the Actor* by Michael Chekhov, Simon Callow writes:

> 'At the beginning of the twenty-first century, we are in the throes of a crisis in theatre acting. It is clearly not a crisis in talent . . . The stars are younger, their bodies are in better condition, they apply themselves energetically

to all the physical aspects of the job. But something isn't happening. Audiences feel it, actors feel it. Disappointment is in the air. The theatre isn't delivering.'

Audience numbers are falling, theatres are closing, and people talk wistfully about a golden age, just after the war, when Olivier and Richardson and Gielgud prowled our main stages and everything was exciting and monumental. Nostalgia might be blurring our perceptions, of course, but the nagging questions remain: is theatre dying? Is it just changing? Are we missing something?

I appreciate that there are many reasons why theatre seems to be declining. Simon Callow seems to feel that it might be something about the style of acting practised by today's generation of actors. But is there more to it than that? Influential theatre practitioners like Peter Brook and Jerzy Grotowski have talked about theatre in quasi-spiritual terms: the need for 'Holy Theatre' and 'Sacred Actors'. Their use of the terms is not Christian but they both sense that theatre should have 'something more' than we see today. For example, in his book *There Are No Secrets*, Brook writes:

'Regarding "Holy Theatre", the essential thing is to recognize that there is an invisible world which needs to be made visible.'

I agree with this, but the problem is that the theatre doesn't know what that 'invisible world' is.

And then we have the church. How to describe the church today? Of course, there are many different kinds of churches, just as there are many different kinds of theatre. But if I asked you the question: does the church seem more or less relevant than it did fifty years ago, what would you say? Are congregation numbers rising, or falling? Do our grandparents look back to a golden age when the church seemed more important? Are our churches impressive, monumental and increasingly ignored? So I ask again: is church dying? Is it just changing? Are we missing something?

Of course, you might argue that 'popularity' and 'importance' are worldly measures and not a true gauge of a successful church. The early church was certainly not popular – in terms of numbers, it was tiny. But when we read about the early church, it certainly seems relevant to its culture, doesn't it? It seems radical. Do we, as a church, have that kind of effect today?

My intention here is not to be judgemental or cynical. I am perfectly aware that there are brilliant churches in the UK today. But I still argue that the Church with a capital 'C' is easy to ignore. The image the church as a whole has is not that of a radical, revolutionary or relevant spiritual body, but rather of a fuddy-duddy, kill-joy, establishment figure.

However, there are still some times when the church is demonstrably popular and necessary, just as there are times when the theatre is clearly popular and necessary. One of those times is Christmas. At Christmas our theatres and our churches are full.

Christmas

In church, congregations sing together, in the semi-darkness of candlelight, often joining in with liturgical phrases as they listen to familiar stories of the birth of Jesus Christ.

In the theatre, audiences sit in the near darkness of the stalls and the galleries, often joining together in shouting well-known phrases or singing songs, as they listen to traditional stories told in a broadly familiar way.

Other similarities include the specialist workers that both church and theatre require to lead the group of people through the ceremony; in the church this is the vicar or leadership team and in the theatre it is the actors. Both events might well involve some kind of food. Often mince pies and mulled wine are available at carol services while sweets are thrown to the audiences at the pantomime and there is a well-stocked bar for the interval. When everything goes well, audiences and congregations leave both places feeling a little bit better than when they went in. There is a powerful sense of community about both events and strong stories are at the heart of them too.

That is surely where the similarities end, though, for the tone of the two events is quite different. An evening at a carol service will probably be marked by a sense of beauty: the candlelight, the building, the songs and the story itself lend themselves to a kind of hush and a feeling of peace. In contrast, the evening at a pantomime is characterized by riotous laughter, irreverent humour, bright colours, ridiculous characters, in-jokes and slapstick.

The tone of the carol service is reverent; the pantomime is irreverent. People should leave the service more peaceful and contented than when they went in, and leave the theatre still laughing and feeling a little bit more alive. These are two events with a great deal in common, but which differ greatly in tone and in their effect on their audience.

It may be that we wish that these two events were not so popular, or that people saw other kinds of theatre besides pantomime and came to services besides 'carols by candlelight'. Possibly both events are viewed by regular theatre and church attendees as rather crude examples of their respective forms. It could, quite reasonably, be pointed out that just because something is well attended does not necessarily mean that something is good. Nevertheless, crude or not, they are enduringly popular, so my suspicion is that they meet a need. What might this be?

I think the carol service explores and celebrates who God is, and the pantomime explores and celebrates humanity – and people need to do both.

This is disputable, I realize. Perhaps people go purely out of a sense of tradition, but there have been many other 'traditional' events that have fallen from favour, so I maintain that these two events provide something that on some level is essential.

A Family Resemblance

In any case, these two events represent church and theatre at their most popular in the UK at the start of the twenty-first century. Perhaps it should come as no surprise that they have so much in common, for the church and the theatre are, after all, father and son.

The origins of theatre are religious and, in Europe at least, decisively shaped by the Christian church. No wonder they share so many features – it is a family resemblance.

Perhaps their differences should not surprise us either for, like so many modern families, they have become polarized and estranged.

There is a picture hanging in my parents' house (not, I'm happy to say, representative of their views) entitled 'The Broad and Narrow Way'. If you look closely at the picture you will see that on the 'Broad Way' there is a theatre and on the 'Narrow Way' there is a church. The message is fairly clear – if you go to or (heaven forbid) work in the theatre it will probably be fun, but you will go to hell. If you go to church there will be no fun, but you will end up in heaven.

This picture sums up much of the church's historical dealings with the theatre. The theatre, particularly since the Reformation, has been seen as trivial, frivolous and, in the final analysis, sinful. Thankfully, this perception seems to be slowly changing.

The theatre itself has done little to endear itself to the church for centuries, preferring instead to largely characterize its erstwhile parent in numerous plays as a succession of dim-witted, absent-minded and benign but ultimately irrelevant vicars. Also, (much though as a professional theatre worker I might like to deny it) there is no doubt that over the years the theatre has celebrated sinfulness. The basic premise of Restoration comedy, for example, seems to be that adultery (or at least the idea of adultery) is funny. The church was never likely to go along with that! Again, thankfully, that period in theatre's history is over. Now spirituality is back on the agenda.

In a sense, the pantomime and carol service represent the best and worst of what the theatre and the church have to offer. The pantomime is funny and colourful, but trivial and lightweight. The carol service is beautiful and peaceful, but humourless. I believe it is possible to produce theatre that has raucous, riotous humanity as well as the moments of stillness and awe that come from knowing a holy God. To put it another way, I think that the carol service and the pantomime can be brought together. I believe this because I've seen it happen, and I believe it because when I look at history, I see that it's happened before.

Two

The Mystery Plays and the End of the Cycle

To look at the kind of theatre I have been talking about we have to go back a long way, right back to the Middle Ages. Before we do, though, I would like to say just one thing by way of introduction to this chapter: the point of this book is to encourage theatre within the church. The early church dramas were created before such things as copyright law were brought in, so if I describe a technique or a feature of the drama that you like, might I respectfully encourage you to borrow it? Adapt it, reuse it, make it work for you – that's the point. With that understood, let's get back to the Middle Ages.

At this time, British church services were conducted in Latin, a foreign language to the Saxon population. The Bible was not available to the common people and, in any case, the population was largely illiterate.

In addition to this, although Christianity was un-challenged as the dominant religion, it coexisted along-side numerous superstitions and remnants of pagan belief. This presented a problem when it came to teaching people Christian doctrine.

Interestingly, similar problems face the church today. The majority of the population of the UK may be able to read but (generally) they don't read the Bible. And although many of them, if pushed, would describe themselves as Christians, the actual gospel message and biblical doctrine is, at best, only hazily understood.

Church Drama Begins

The tenth-century church responded to these problems with a sophisticated use of the available resources, becoming expert at using imagery to visually communicate its message to the population.

For example, throughout the year a cross would be prominently displayed on a high beam in the church – a visual reminder of Christ's sacrifice. Then, on Good Friday, this cross would be taken down from its position and laid either on the north side of the altar or in what was known as the Easter Sepulchre, an existing or specially constructed tomb, where it would rest covered with a white cloth. There the cross would remain, with men keeping vigil around it, until Easter Sunday when it would 'rise again' back to its exalted station. In this way, the story of the death and resurrection of Jesus was related visually.

This may not sound terribly exciting, but these visual metaphors quickly evolved into something a little more complex and substantial when the priests themselves took part in re-enacting scenes from the gospel.

Try to imagine what it might have been like to be a part of the congregation during this next early drama, which tells the story of the women discovering the angel at the empty tomb.

Male priests, specially costumed for their roles, enter the church as if to take part in the service. One of them, dressed in white, is seated in the sepulchre. The remaining three (representing the women) are coming to anoint the body. They are carrying censers of incense. They swing the censers as they approach the tomb and the smell of the incense permeates the church. Suddenly the women encounter the angel. As an audience we may not be able to follow the precise meaning of the dialogue but we can see from the consternation of the women that something very unexpected has happened. The dialogue is sung between the women and the angel until at last the angel sings 'He is not here, he is risen' and as he does so the church bells suddenly ring out. Curtain, bows, rave review in *The Times*.

All right, to the modern reader this doesn't immediately suggest a West End hit, but it has more complexity than you might at first think.

When the 'angel' indicated the empty grave clothes in this drama he used the same white cloth which only the day before had covered the cross (now restored to its position on the beam). So this little drama does not replace the earlier visual aid, but develops and elaborates on it. There are layers of meaning at work in this simple play, all reinforcing and informing one another.

It may not be great art, but what we have here is the beginning of a theatre. It has a script, stage directions, costumes, imagery and even elements of total theatre as the senses of the congregation are stimulated through the use of incense, pageantry, music and sound effects.

Clearly, it is also an attempt to make the invisible visible. These early dramatists are trying to communicate a moment of profound holy awe.

To modern sensibilities it still sounds fairly crude; however, I would ask one question:

How many churches today do as much to help their congregations understand on an emotional and sensory level?

The drama may not be sophisticated (the dialogue was all sung and still in Latin) but the church was using the resources it had. These were not professional actors, but ordinary church workers simply doing their best because they wanted to communicate.

To return for a moment to our modern 'carols by candlelight' service, we can see that many of the elements of this early drama are still used to this day. We still have the music and the sensory stimulation of the smell of the candles alongside the visual metaphor of the light in the darkness. In many ways, it doesn't seem surprising that these services are well attended. Of course they are traditional, but churches also go to far more effort for them. It seems to me that this is the one church service that retains the total theatre aspects pioneered by the medieval church.

The Drama Develops

To return to our brief history – things quickly developed from this simple drama. Before long, short plays were being performed, leading congregations from one part of the church to the other as the location of each scene changed. This promenade style of performance would continue to be characteristic of medieval theatre.

The promenade technique allows the actors to stage their scenes in the most appropriate parts of the church, making their meaning clearer and their impact greater, and it also helps to maintain the interest of the audience if their point of focus and relationship with the actors keeps changing.

Again, I might ask how many churches today would think to move their congregations around to change the dynamic between the communicators and those they are communicating with. Fixed pews make this kind of thing tricky in many church buildings, but if yours allows it, why not give it a try? Experiment with different relationships between the actors and the audience: you'll find it can make quite a striking difference to the experience.

Techniques that the professional theatre would not adopt for centuries, such as theatre-in-the-round, were developed in these church performances and it all came from a desire to express and share stories to the best of their ability.

You might reasonably argue, 'Surely the reason these dramas were developing was because the people couldn't understand the Latin services, whereas we conduct our services in English so everyone already understands.'

Indeed, the acts of theatre that we have been discussing were all performed in Latin, as they were all part of the normal church service. Therefore, their intelligibility rested on their symbolic imagery and sensory effects rather than their dialogue. However, when these simple dramas did start to use the vernacular we see that they become more elaborate, not less. To the medieval mind, using language that was intellectually understood by the populace was plainly not in itself enough, and so over many years the church of the Middle Ages (and beyond) evolved its theatre until it became what we now call the 'mystery cycle'.

The Mystery Cycle

The mystery cycle was a series of short plays that told the biblical story from creation to judgement. From around 1325 mystery cycles were performed in many different towns. Sadly, many of the scripts have been lost to us. However, we have a number of surviving plays, including the complete cycles from York and Chester, which can tell us a great deal about what these performances might have been like. Francis Edwards' book *Ritual and Drama: the Mediaeval Theatre* (Cambridge: The Lutterworth Press, 1976) is excellent for a more in-depth look at the medieval theatre.

The mystery plays were performed on feast days (typically the feast of Corpus Christi). These plays were no longer confined to the church building but were instead performed on multiple stages around a town. The audience could walk from one to the next seeing different parts of the story told by different actors. Again, we can see from this how an idea had been put into practice during the promenade-style performances within the church building, and then developed and expanded to encompass the whole town or town centre.

By now production of these plays had become too much work for the church to manage alone, and had been handed over to the trade guilds to perform. Indeed, the term 'mystery' perhaps referred to the 'mysteries' or craft of the guilds, so these are plays performed by craftsmen. The church would continue to perform their own drama as part of the church services, and now the mystery plays of the guilds would form an integral and hugely popular part of the religious festivals.

So what were the plays like and what can we learn from them?

It is only fair to point out that the medieval plays had a particular advantage over any church theatre produced nowadays. This advantage lay in the fact that the plays were expressing a worldview universally held by their audience. This shared viewpoint meant that what the audience saw on stage were representations of their dearest beliefs, their greatest hopes and their darkest fears. So there was a kind of vested interest in the plays that went beyond the natural charm of their narrative. This meant that the plays were popular in the truest sense of the word. They were plays by the people, performed for the people, about things that the people cared about. We can perhaps recreate this kind of feeling when we perform in church, but if we were to take the plays onto the streets of our towns today we could not hope for the same unanimity in our audiences.

We can, however, recapture an aspect of this 'popular' quality if we look beyond the walls of our churches for our actors. We can involve amateur groups, children and anyone else who would like to perform these plays for a wide audience. This will bring in a varied range of friends and parents who are there to support the actors. This feeling of mutual support must have been a feature of these early plays, as the actors would inevitably be performing for people they knew.

The second aspect to consider about the plays was that they were visually spectacular. The guilds went to considerable expense to achieve pyrotechnic effects for the devils. They often used highly decorated wagons as their stages, travelling through the towns to various performance stations where they would enact their part of the story. The natural elements were used to their advantage as well. For example, we know that the York Cycle began with the story of creation and that it would be scheduled to begin at dawn. This meant that the actor playing God would be speaking his lines regarding the making of the world, of day and of night, just as the sun was rising. This must have been an awe-inspiring moment.

We also know that the guilds took great pride in achieving a high artistic standard, as we have records of actors being fined for fluffing their lines. The pride of the guilds was on the line and they seemed to have taken this very seriously.

I would suggest that there is no reason why this same pride in the artistic standard of our work might not apply to us as well. We should not necessarily go around fining people whenever they make a mistake, but we should aim to do our very best with our performances.

Significantly, the language of the plays was suited to their function. Anyone who has performed or spoken publicly outside knows that doing so brings certain challenges. Chief amongst these is that it is hard, even for trained actors, to make themselves heard. The voice tends to float away on the wind. But the mystery plays use particular techniques to help the actor with this: they are written, for the most part, in rhyming and alliterative verse. This is very helpful as the ear of the audience becomes attuned to the rhythm, making it seem easier to hear. So, to return to the beginning of the York Cycle, we can imagine seeing the sun rising as we hear God saying:

'*Ego sum Alpha et Omega: vita, via, veritas, primus*
  et novissimus.
I am gracious and great, God without beginning,
I am maker unmade, all might is in me,
I am life, and way unto wealth-winning
I am foremost and first, as I bid shall it be.'

The alliteration of 'gracious' with 'great' and 'maker unmade' with 'might' is particularly suited to being heard outside: they are hard sounds that travel well.

Also, it's worth noticing that the actor is talking directly to the audience. This makes it easier for people to hear and has the effect of actively engaging them in the play. There is no imaginary 'fourth wall' between the actor and the audience in this theatre, nor is there any pretence that the action on stage is really happening; this is a play that acknowledges its audience and talks directly to them.

In a moment I will be looking at how the mystery plays use irreverence to celebrate humanity in the face of great and terrible events, but here the dramatist has deliberately linked the beginning of the play to the church. The first line is in Latin: the language of the clergy and the Bible. It is a reverent moment designed to inspire respect.

This leads me on to the final point I'd like to make about the mystery plays. Stylistically, they were extremely varied. Returning again to my original comparison, we might call moments like this from the 'creation play' the 'carols by candlelight' end of the spectrum, a way of celebrating and glorifying God. However, as I have hinted, the mystery cycle also contained elements closer to the pantomime which celebrated humanity, at times irreverently.

For example, in the middle of the section on the flood in the Chester Cycle there is a reasonably large part focusing on domestic strife between Noah and his wife. Noah is characterized as a rather aged husband burdened with a remarkably shrewish wife who is reluctant to leave her friends even when faced with the terrible flood. It even descends into knockabout farce as she is finally dragged on board the Ark only to respond by giving her husband a good clip round the ear. Even to a modern reader or audience member the scene is amusing. Amusing or not, though, it's a fairly rough way of dramatically representing a major biblical character.

There is another similarity to the pantomime in this play. In the York version this part of the cycle was performed by the Guild of Shipwrights and there is an amusing transformation that occurs in Noah as, aided by God's grace, he changes in his language from being an Old Testament character amazed by God's commands and ignorant of shipbuilding, to an adroit medieval shipwright using the terminology of his trade. To the audience of the time this was probably very funny too.

And yet the flood itself is a terrible story of judgement that nevertheless contains within it God's mercy and salvation. So why are there these elements of humour? To modern sensibilities they can seem terribly inappropriate. What effect do they have? What were the medieval writers thinking when they included these passages?

It is worth bearing in mind that life for the average audience member in the Middle Ages was very different from today. Life expectancy was much lower and the people were dependent upon the weather and the harvest each year in order to survive. This meant that death was a day-to-day presence and consequently issues of damnation and salvation were very relevant. Something like a huge flood, for instance, would be the kind of thing that they greatly feared. This state of living at the mercy of the elements seems to have created a kind of gallows humour that is reflected in the art that they produced. There was no need for the medieval writer to drive home the seriousness of the flood or any other part of the story – his audience already knew it was serious. Instead, the writers of the time seem to have seized the opportunity to laugh in the face of death and enjoy being alive while they could.

For the church today, things are a little different and consequently we may choose to approach things in a different way in our performances. But before we dismiss the humour of the mystery plays out of hand, let's have a look to see whether it might serve another function or teach us something of value.

I would suggest that the unexpectedly funny sections of the plays accomplish a number of things. For a start, they bring the stories down to earth. We all know about domestic problems and so it can help us to connect with the story to see that Noah had problems with his wife too. It isn't very politically correct, but it could be very funny! It also helps us to see Noah not as an untouchable and holy figure but as a man like the rest of us. Similarly, the in-joke of the shipwright's vocabulary in the mouth of an Old Testament patriarch becomes amusing when you remember that it is the shipwrights themselves presenting this section of the cycle: it's just like the references to popular culture that litter the modern pantomime. It grounds the story in some common experience that helps us to connect with the characters and feel that they are a little bit more like us.

Perhaps even more importantly, though, changes in tone help us to listen. In my experience, if something is quiet and reverent for too long then the audience stops listening and becomes bored. Changes in tone keep an audience on their toes and the humour seems more effective by contrast with the serious sections, and vice versa. Indeed, as a performer I sometimes feel that you need to earn the audience's attention and that making them laugh is one way of doing this. If you can make an audience laugh, especially in the early sections of a play, then you have a much better chance of making them really listen later on. So we can laugh along as Noah's wife wants to stay with her friends but the laughter stops as the flood comes and her friends are washed away.

The mystery plays often have a quality of humour about them that, in the end, does not diminish the story that they depict. Indeed, what they appear to have accomplished at the time (and indeed when they have been revived) is a wonderful combination of the rough pantomime-like theatre of the people with moments of true reverence and awe.

The End of the Cycle

I sometimes wonder whether the mystery plays evolved as far as they could, or if there was more to come. My own feeling is that they contained the DNA of great theatre; they were funny and moving and ambitious in scope. They were still crude in some respects and the verse form that they used can seem bombastic and naïve, unsuited to realistic dialogue, but then their performance conditions would have required a robust energy above all so it is hard to fault them for that. It is galling though to remember that the theatre of the Renaissance produced some of the greatest plays ever written, and was directly influenced by the mystery play tradition, yet the content could not be Christian due to the legislation at the time. What might Shakespeare have produced had he been allowed to talk directly about God?

Sadly, as I have already mentioned, the mystery plays were the furthest that the church and the theatre were to develop together. The Reformation brought us many wonderful things, but the Puritans did not look kindly on theatre or art in general and the two institutions have remained divorced ever since.

In England the changes began under the reign of Henry VIII who, largely for political reasons, found himself aligned with German Lutheran princes and therefore more tolerant of their ideas. Doctrinally this radically changed the traditional church teachings. Some of the changes were forced upon the church in the shape of Injunctions in 1536, 1538 and again in 1547. These had many different ramifications, one of which was the abolition of some feast days on the grounds that they promoted vice and idleness. Of course, with the feast days gone the theatre that had been performed at the celebrations went too.

But the damage done to the theatre of the time was not just a by-product of other legislation. It represented real hostility on the part of the Puritans. There were four main strands to the Puritan objections to the theatre.

To begin with, the Church Fathers had spoken out against the Roman theatre and the Reformers seemed to extend their objections to encompass theatre as a whole.

The mystery plays themselves had evolved partly as a means to communicate a doctrine that had been shaped by the Catholic Church. Consequently, the Puritans were opposed to them. It's worth remembering at this point that although today we tend to focus on tolerance and the beliefs that Catholics and Protestants have in common; in the sixteenth century people were dying for these doctrinal differences.

As the plays were performed on feast days no doubt there was a certain amount of revelry and drunkenness that accompanied them, and the Puritans took that sort of thing very seriously.

Finally, the Reformed church seemed to view theatre in the same light as they viewed many of the religious statues and images – as tantamount to idolatry. The injunctions particularly targeted the images within the church. Even today, I have heard the second commandment used to attack a play (actually, it was *Emma's Mystery* – one of the plays in this volume) that depicted Jesus on stage. My critic's point was that to put the Son of God on the stage is an inherently blasphemous notion and nothing I could say would convince him otherwise. Looking back, I'm not really sure why he came to see that particular play.

The concerns of the Reformers are worthy of serious consideration even if we don't agree with them. There surely is a danger in representing God on stage; after all, we could make a character say anything. So we have to approach this aspect of our art with care, respect and awe. Catholic theology is clearly embedded within the mystery cycle. My own feeling is that the Puritans could have reformed the theology rather than abolish the theatre. And the Church Fathers may well have regarded the Roman theatre as sinful; it may well have *been* sinful – I just don't believe that has to extend to all theatre.

In the course of researching this chapter it has become clearer to me that the suppression of the theatre was a gradual and haphazard process rather than a coherent policy. The Puritans were trying to reform the church and mould it into what they believed God wanted it to be. I can't fault that aim but it had some consequences that I deeply regret. Their opposition to the theatre reached its apotheosis when in 1642 the Puritan authorities banned the performance of all plays within the London city limits. The theatres remained closed for the next eighteen years, only reopening with the restoration of the monarchy.

The Bible teaches that humanity was made in the image of God. If God is the creator than it stands to reason that people will be creative too. The Puritans could never stop this creativity. Sadly, all that they achieved was to deny the church any kind of voice within the performing arts. The theatre that characterized the period of the Restoration, in my opinion, justified many of the Puritan concerns and fears in a manner that appears almost deliberate. The Restoration comedies are sparklingly witty, frivolous, obsessed with sex and adultery and appear as though they are a reaction against a starchy Puritan aesthetic.

It seemed as though church theatre was dead and that God within the theatre was dead too. As we shall see, though, this position was to be remarkably reversed.

Three

The State of Play

When, as a young man, I decided that I wanted to be an actor, I had visions of playing leading classical roles on the grandest stages of the land, or heroic parts in Hollywood movies. Each night, as I lay on my bed, I would imagine scenes of incredible success. I often fell asleep quietly mouthing some variation of the phrase 'I'd like to thank the Academy'. These dreams were destined to remain unfulfilled, but over time would be transformed into something totally different.

I left university, intending to pursue my ambitions to the best of my ability, and immediately started working for a Christian theatre company. I stayed with this company for about eighteen months. Then I became a freelance actor and did a variety of badly-paid performances of Shakespeare plays to aggressive teenagers for about six months, before I started working for another Christian theatre company where I have been ever since.

I appreciate that, as actor's memoirs go, this isn't the most gripping one you'll ever read, but I include it here to make one important point: this kind of career would simply not have been possible as little as thirty years ago. In recent times, Christian theatre companies have become part of the theatrical landscape of this country: not a large or prestigious part, but a part nonetheless.

When we look back at the history of the church and the theatre this is a remarkable turnaround. To try to understand how this could have happened and what the current position of Christian theatre is, I interviewed the Artistic Directors of two of the biggest and best-known professional Christian theatre companies in the country, who also happen to be two of my most recent employers: Paul Burbridge of Riding Lights Theatre Company, and David Robinson of Saltmine Theatre Company.

Riding Lights

Riding Lights were the company that I joined almost straight from university, but I have been aware of them for most of my life. Formed in 1977 in York, they have performed a wide selection of material over their lifetime – from short sketches to Shakespeare plays – and received considerable acclaim from secular critics as well as from within the church. In 1992 they formed Riding Lights Roughshod, which is made up of companies of young actors recruited each year to perform in local community contexts, going into schools and prisons as well as churches. In 1999 Riding Lights opened their own theatre: the Friargate Theatre in York.

Paul Burbridge founded Riding Lights Theatre Company with his childhood friend Murray Watts, and has continued to oversee their work in his role as Artistic Director. Initially well-known as an actor and writer, Paul has since directed scores of productions. The sketches that he and Murray wrote have been published in several books and many of these have become staples for Christian drama groups. I interviewed Paul at his York home in late September of 2008.

Was there a Christian theatre scene when Riding Lights started?

I think we came into a church world that was beginning to be aware of the arts. There was a groundswell of 'charismatic renewal' people who were more open to the arts, and the ways in which Christian mission could be decorated or enhanced by people using their gifts.

How did Riding Lights start?

I met David Watson, who was a key communicator himself and very interested in the arts, at Oxford when he came to do a university mission. I did some monologues for him at this mission and from that I struck up a relationship with David that was crucial for Riding Lights.

It meant that at the end of university I found myself up here [in York] living in David's house in the community, working with him at the church and beginning to put practical flesh on the bones of ideas that I'd had with Murray [Watts – co-founder of Riding Lights] since we were teenagers really, as a boys' dream. It was beginning to make sense because here was a church that had a radical view in terms of outreach and setting people free to do what they were good at, and they were quite happy to support a theatre company, so it came together and all those things were given to us. We were allowed to do what we wanted to do.

The precursor to Riding Lights was some contacts we made at Scripture Union. Murray had been invited to run the youth work at a beach mission that we'd both been to as kids, and he decided to get something together with student friends and do Bible stories as street theatre around the town. We were called Breadrock, and we did that for three summers – really learning what street theatre was all about. Then we started to get invitations to big things: conferences and venues like the Albert Hall, so we actually found a way of showing what Breadrock could do to enormous numbers of people who would then try to book us, and we weren't available to do the bookings because I was either in York or doing a year at theological college. So, really, by the time I was finishing the theological college year and was free to start a professional company all those various bits were in place.

There was a market for it and there was a church willing to support us so the whole thing could start. Then of course it quickly got further publicity through the big city-wide missions that David Watson was leading, where we were by ourselves on the platform in front of a lot of people who suddenly *got it*. They saw Christians doing biblical sketches: there would be a speaker, then a sketch which was usually just a lightweight cartoon or revue type comedy, maybe based on a parable, with some music and dance – and the whole thing was like a seedbed.

How has the performance material changed?

I think we got to the stage four or five years ago when we realized that the specifically biblical sketch material was becoming less and less useful, because the people we were performing to were less and less versed in Bible stories. It didn't make any sense, so what we started to do was to say 'What are the themes, what

are the ideas, what are the values behind those stories?'
And then we began to look for a repertoire of stories
that contained something true. Those stories were from
literature, the Bible, Shakespeare, myths and legends,
and also personal stories from the cast members of
Roughshod.

So we've taken a cue from the world that we live
in: we do more stories now and less of the funny
biblical sketches. There was a feeling that we were
also a little bit sick of the sketches and the kind of
Christian confectionery that can be. You need more
meat, something a bit more solid.

So now we're trying to bring what we have to bear
on the issues of the day a bit more. Often we're working
in partnership with other organizations that may have
a particular purpose. People who want us to work with
them are suggesting subjects for plays. That has been
really good because you realize that there's nothing in
the world of human thought that is out of reach. So we
could do a play about science, for instance and then
people want to talk about ethical issues, biogenetics,
and what Christians think about this. And you realize
that's really important, and that a play is a perfect
vehicle to explore really difficult issues that you can't
get up and necessarily spout about in the pulpit, but if
you can articulate them well, even in a confrontational
way, through characters in a play, (and people don't
think that you are necessarily espousing everything
that character is saying) it allows a debate to happen.
That's great, that's happening all the time.

It's like that myth of the Renaissance person who's
interested in everything – you really do have to be
prepared to get involved, whatever the subject is you
have to go in and try and understand it. That's been
invigorating.

In terms of how you are perceived, was there any problem moving from the sketch and revue type material to more serious work?

Yes, I think so. We do far more work now than we ever did in those early years and it's far more diverse, but we still have people coming up and saying 'Are you still going? We thought you'd died out after the work with David Watson.' There is still a legacy of that era with David: 'Time to Act' and 'Lightning Sketches' [Riding Lights publications of sketches] and that sort of exposure that we had then. That is certainly the image that people have had of Riding Lights.

Now the bigger challenge for us is the new church people who don't share any of that experience with us, or who belong to churches that are largely Riding Lights free. The new generation don't know us, and we want to be a resource to them, to get alongside them and their young people particularly, and so we need to break into that market.

But we do see the importance of being out there in the secular context more than in the church. I know that we are still very dependent on Christian support but even when churches want Roughshod we're asking them to find performances in the secular world for the team, not just in the church.

You spoke of a groundswell of the arts within the church when Riding Lights started. Is that still happening? Where are we in the church now in terms of drama?

I feel there's been a huge sea-change in terms of people getting into the arts, and people setting up courses like you're doing [at the time of this interview I was working with Regents College to create a joint degree course in Applied Theology and the Performing Arts] is evidence of that. That wasn't around at all thirty years ago. At that time there were very, very few people who would admit to being Christians coming out of drama schools or looking for the kind of work that we were setting up. Now there are many more people who recognize that for all kinds of reasons drama is a fantastic subject; a really key subject in schools. And within the church I feel that Riding Lights in a small way has helped to create an argument that shows that theatre is good, solid; it's a grown-up thing to do. It's not just running round in silly hats! I think that has changed.

But the church has always been very faddish. Theatre has been much more flavour-of-the-month than it is now. Churches blow hot and cold on whether they have time for a drama group. I think the trouble with plays is that they are too open-ended for most people in a church; they're too risky; there's a danger as they don't tell people what to think, but they feel they ought to be told what to think! So they blow very hot and cold and I don't know what the state is at the moment.

And the future?

Sometimes you don't know where you're going but you've got to keep going in such a way that your work remains relevant. I've always had that attitude to guidance: you can only guide something when it's moving, it's about momentum. You have to keep pushing ahead even though you're absolutely not in control of trends in the church or in society, but you believe in what you're doing, and you believe that it's important to exercise people's imaginations, which happens less and less.

But when you do get a show that does do it – that does go into prison or go into school, then you see what theatre is all about, which is the wonderful chemistry of the human contact and that is very precious. So we shouldn't be so overwhelmed by trends that we lose that.

Saltmine

Saltmine Theatre Company has been going since 1985. They have grown from a small sketch team to a company capable of mounting full-scale productions in secular theatres across the country. They have received awards at the Edinburgh Festival Fringe and been invited to take part in the Royal Shakespeare Company's visitors' season.

David Robinson joined the company in 1989 and has spearheaded the artistic development of Saltmine's work. He has become well-known to Christian audiences particularly though his comic talents as actor and writer. His first book, *Three Wise Men and a Baby*, was published by Authentic Media in 2008. David has directed many of Saltmine's recent productions and he has also acted as the artistic coordinator at Spring Harvest. I spoke to him in Saltmine's hometown of Dudley in October of 2008.

Did your church background encourage you to perform? Were you able to perform in your church?

Yes, I formed a company called Lifeline in my church with two or three others and that's where my writing started. It was very simple, and not very good when I look back at it now! We had some musicians as well, so it was a mixture of drama and music. Then Chrysalis was a creative arts organization that began at my church that I've helped by writing for them. So my church was very supportive of the creative arts and has hosted full-length productions in recent years, so they've been a big help.

When I first went to my minister and said 'I think I want to go into full-time Christian work as an actor,' he arranged a meeting for me with Nigel Goodwin [of the Arts Centre Group] in London and his very wonderful, over the top, enthusiastic remarks just encouraged me to keep going, really! And a nice moment was that he came to see *The Screwtape Letters* at Stratford some years later and so saw some of the dream being developed. I guess if someone at college had asked me what my dream was, it was to run my own theatre company and that's basically what I've been doing.

Did you train in the performing arts?

I did, and then I went on to do arts administration in London, which stood me in good stead because then I went straight on to Covent Garden to work at the Opera House in their marketing department. Here at Saltmine some months it's all admin for me so it's been a help. I wouldn't say it's my most comfortable area but I can do it. Performing is where I'm most comfortable, or just being in that performance atmosphere and seeing new productions come together and being part of that process.

How did you join Saltmine?

I joined Saltmine in the summer of 1989. I'd been to Spring Harvest [a Christian conference] the previous

April and had felt quite strongly that God was telling me to get involved in full-time Christian work, and in fact I talked to some of the Saltmine folk after one of the meetings there in Minehead. Dave Pope was in charge of Saltmine at the time, and I talked briefly to him, though he wasn't aware of any vacancies then.

But later on I wrote to Saltmine and by then there was a vacancy within the theatre company. I auditioned a couple of times [Saltmine require applicants to go through two auditions before they select new actors] and got in. I travelled to the family holiday that Saltmine ran in Suffolk and joined the theatre company.

Straightaway, almost from arriving there, I began to rehearse sketches. It was sort of 'Learn this sketch and you're on tomorrow' so not much change there! A schools play on prejudice was running called *Snide and Prejudice* and that had bookings for September, so we were there for three weeks then we had our own holiday and then we were coming back to schools.

And that really, was the pattern: sketches and a schools play, schools play and sketches. We didn't work on our own very much; generally we were supporting our national evangelists who were touring round leading church-based missions. My diary would be back-to-back missions sometimes and that could involve going to all sorts of events through the week, an old people's home, a mums and toddlers church service, possibly a drama workshop, and then they would get us into schools and we would do this forty-minute presentation and maybe a workshop afterwards, but there were no full-length plays in the evening or anything like that. And that was what I did for a couple of years.

Towards the end of that period we developed a play called *The Big Screen Life of Humphrey Barton* that we offered to churches as sort of an opening night to the mission. It was a very evangelism-friendly event, nothing too heavy, about this guy who lived a 'Billy Liar' style life, living through films. It was good fun and proved pretty popular, and that was when things started to change as we extended the sketches into something a bit longer.

Then I was offered the leadership of the company two years after touring as a team member, which I accepted, but I proposed to the directors that we did more of the *Humphrey Barton* type material, more full-length stuff, especially more full-length TIE [Theatre in Education] material and more touring on our own so that we weren't dependent on the evangelists all the time, but were allowed so many months of the year to do our own thing.

This was risky at the time because we weren't known for that kind of thing, and it was hard work to get a full house at Spring Harvest, and to encourage churches to say 'What about a theatre night?' So we sent the script back to Alan [MacDonald, of Footprints Theatre Company, who had written the *Humphrey Barton* script] and asked if he could develop this into a two-hour play, suitable to go into arts centres and small theatres as well as (more commonly on that first tour) big churches. And that's what happened.

We had a very fortunate moment when we did a mission in Stratford-upon-Avon and spoke to people who worked for the Royal Shakespeare Company at The Swan [one of the Royal Shakespeare Company's theatres], and they got us into their annual visitors' season with *Humphrey Barton*. That kicked us off really. We could put it on our publicity and show that we were ranked alongside other small-scale touring companies. And that's where the full-length plays developed, really. *Christ in the Concrete City* came after and then the watershed was *Screwtape Letters*, which was our third main production.

Why did you want to develop the material beyond the sketches?

I felt we were attracting good quality actors who I wanted to keep, and I felt that a way of keeping them was to make a statement that they were joining a *theatre* company: so yes, we are mission orientated and communicating Christ is at the heart of what Saltmine is, but we've got talented, creative, trained actors whose desire is to act for Christ and to use their skills and their faith combined in very effective ways.

And I think that sketches can be effective – I'm not decrying that – but I really felt that we could be offering something else to churches, outside their own buildings, in a theatre setting. And I knew it would take a while, but by the time of *Screwtape* in 1994 we were just about getting there.

What do you think is the value of the material you perform that isn't evangelistic but aimed at a church audience?

I guess it's similar to a preacher who is preaching to the converted. We are teaching them and seeking to disciple them, trying to open their eyes to something new. I would hope that the material that I write and you write for that clientele does move them on in their faith in some way.

And I also think that churches are our customers and our biggest supporters, so of course some of our material will be specifically for them. We hope that it does challenge them, we hope that they are not always one hundred per cent comfortable with it, but that it is an enjoyable experience and that when we say something like 'Next year we're coming with something evangelistic to your local theatre, and we want you to bring your friends and family and work colleagues to *The Cross and the Switchblade*', that they would trust us and come with us.

I feel it would be going in the wrong direction to cut the church and its audience out of our calendar, I think we would struggle with that. We would not be here without them – we couldn't go to any town in this country without a church getting behind us in some way.

How has the work developed since *Screwtape* in 1994?

I feel quite strongly that we should improve with each major production and that although we're never going to reach perfection, we should always be aiming for it. So I would hope that we are now seen as a creative organization that does deliver good quality full-length productions that would stand alongside any other touring theatre companies that go to any provincial theatre in this country. And indeed the proof of that is that some of these theatres will ring us and say 'When's your next tour, when are you coming?' because we fill the venues for them. Very often they will add people to their mailing list who they wouldn't see for the rest of the year, so for them we are useful.

But we have moved on from where we were when we first did *Screwtape*. I'd say that the sketch stuff is less important.

We have expanded into what is now, as we speak, four companies, so we are able to cover a wide range of different bookings from all different parts of the Christian family. I've never wanted to align ourselves with any particular branch or denomination and I don't think we have. I think we would happily sit in any church event or conference and that is where we should be.

But I would hope that we could expand further, that we could stay longer at a theatre and that we could fill venues for more than two or three nights. We've talked at length at different times about having some experimental theatre alongside more of an assured box-office winner, so that we can encourage new writers, new performers and new experimental areas of theatre. I can think of a number of people now within the organization who would really love the opportunity to try something new. So if we had a production that could balance that and we knew that one part of the year was going to sell out, then we could allow that to happen, and I would love to see that. I think new writing, new acting and new style is the lifeblood of Saltmine and I guess it's my role to make sure there is space for that to happen.

How has the church climate changed with regards to theatre, from the time that you joined to the present day?

It has changed. I worry that it has reached a bit of a plateau. We went from church halls doing five-minute sketches illustrating a point that an evangelist brought up later, to now where we're at the stage of a church booking us to go into all their local schools in the area, or a church saying 'We want an outreach event this Christmas. Could you come and do it?' We've got nearly eighty performances going out this Christmas.

We've also got churches saying 'When are you next coming to our local theatre? We'll get behind you.' But that has been happening for the last two or three years, if not more.

So I guess I'm wondering 'Where do we go next?' We're just beginning to tease that out. Part of it is providing resources to churches in different ways: with DVDs of our productions, with short films, with scripts and books, and actually equipping them to do it themselves in a better way than maybe they think they can. Even with four companies there's a limit to where we can get to, and probably we're going to go through a phase of putting more back into the church where the creative arts are concerned. I think we're at the stage where they are open to that, and some of the conferences we go to, like Spring Harvest and Keswick Convention, are realizing the importance of the creative arts. The knock-on effect is that the church leaders and the church members who come will pick up on that and want it more. But we just need to get to the stage where churches aren't saying to us 'Come and do it, come and do it, come and do it!' but 'I hear what you're saying, I see these resources and actually you could help us to do it ourselves.' I think that in some strange way will increase the demand for what we do. It might change what we do, but it'll increase it.

Conclusions

In speaking to both David and Paul I was encouraged by the ways in which the church had helped both men in their work setting up and developing professional theatre companies. It seems as though the Pentecostal movement and the subsequent charismatic renewal has changed church perceptions of drama and made Christians more open to theatre as a form of outreach.

Just as the medieval church gave the production of the mystery plays to the trade guilds, the modern church appears to have given professional theatre companies the responsibility for Christian theatre, while the church itself plays the role of patron to the Christian arts. Art has always required patronage as it is expensive to produce and generally not very financially profitable. It has always needed people who value it and are prepared to pay for it.

The danger in this situation is that the one who pays the piper, quite reasonably, expects to call the tune and theatre is generally unhappy about being told which tune to play. As Paul Burbridge mentioned, plays are often disturbingly open-ended and churches can struggle with this aspect of them. As both Riding Lights and Saltmine look to expand the scope of their performance material it will be a challenge to carry the church support with them.

In my experience, churches have no difficulty understanding how theatre can be useful in evangelism or as an aid to the teaching of theological points, but plays often tackle subjects in a very oblique manner, asking questions rather than providing answers and some churches are made uneasy by this lack of dogma. The other side to this problem is that in the secular theatre world, strongly proclaiming the gospel (any gospel, really) results in marginalization and not being taken seriously as an artist. It is important for the professional standing of the Christian theatre companies that they manage to participate in the modern theatrical scene more subtly but that they do so without losing the support of the church. So far, at least, Saltmine and Riding Lights seem to have been able to maintain the church's confidence.

The existence of professional Christian theatre companies is still a recent phenomenon and the progress that Saltmine and Riding Lights have made in that time is impressive. There is still a sense in which they exist outside mainstream theatre, but that may change as they work in partnership with secular groups, as the quality of their work becomes apparent to their peers and as their performance material widens in scope. As I mentioned in the first chapter, the theatre is ready for a new voice to be heard. People are conscious that something is missing, but the hostility that has existed between the church and the theatre will take time before it is forgotten. At the moment Christians in the creative arts are easy to dismiss, so our art needs to be good enough that it is impossible to ignore us. It won't be easy, but I believe that it is vital.

For this to happen the church may have to be tolerant of Christian theatre companies performing plays that have a wider secular appeal, but there is a more important contribution that the church can make.

Drama within the Church

One of the main ways in which the modern church differs from our medieval ancestors is that the church of the Middle Ages continued to use drama in their services, while this seems to have become less common nowadays. Paul Burbridge talked about how theatre has been far more flavour-of-the-month than it is now and David Robinson felt that drama in the church might have reached a plateau. I agree with that assessment. I found myself feeling a little envious as Paul spoke of the 'groundswell' of the arts within the church when Riding Lights started. Sadly, although I accept that the church's attitude has changed positively towards the idea of Christians in the arts in a professional context, I feel a little as though the church has started to lose faith in the idea of drama as part of its services.

This may well be linked to the issue of quality. It can be toe-curling to see a sketch fall flat in church, and rather than risk embarrassment some churches may have simply decided to leave it to the experts. This saddens me a bit as I think that really simple theatrical techniques can enhance a church service, and indeed are already being used in the carol services. I am certain that some of the principles used in this service can easily be extended.

The three-minute sketch that Riding Lights pioneered and that Saltmine have continued to employ really took the church by storm. But the medieval church did not content itself with simple drama; it developed and used all the resources at its disposal. Churches today have far greater resources, but don't use them as creatively. If they did, then church might be a far more compelling experience.

Of course, a church service is an act of worship, not entertainment. But when I look at the medieval church I see the clergy desperate to communicate. Isn't that still the church's job? We communicate more effectively when people *feel* what we're talking about rather than just *hearing* it and for that, their senses and emotions need to be stirred. Theatre is perfect for that.

It does require hard work and dedication, but the payoffs can be massive. As I hope you've seen, the mystery plays evolved out of the work of ordinary, untrained men and women and many of the techniques they use are still effective today. Paul and David both spoke about learning their craft through doing it, when Paul was in Breadrock and David was in Lifeline. I'm certain they tried things that didn't work! I would encourage you to try it as well – you do learn more by directly experiencing live theatre even if your first attempts are not one hundred per cent successful.

Re-awakening the dramatic tradition within the church could have an enormous impact. I'm not talking about some kind of re-enactment (although that could be a starting point) but if preachers and vicars and youth leaders took the power of the stories within the Bible and were able to communicate them in a way that engaged their congregations, the church could be transformed. It would also produce and foster talented people who could go on to use those gifts professionally. As I said in the introduction to this book – it just needs people to try it.

I hope that you will be able to use the plays in this volume to begin to apply some of the techniques we've discussed. But I also hope that you won't stop there, and that you will try to develop these ideas yourselves. There is far more that could be done than I could ever imagine. Only now is the church beginning to pick up where it left off centuries ago, so we have some lost time to make up. But we have the best stories – now all we have to do is tell them.

The Plays

The following scripts are intended to help you to put some of the ideas discussed into practice. Both of the plays in this volume have been inspired to some extent by the mystery cycles of the Middle Ages, although these ideas have been fused with more modern styles of theatre, especially in *Emma's Mystery*.

We'll start with *The Passion Play*, as this is perhaps the more obvious attempt at a modern recreation of a mystery play.

The Passion Play: An Introduction

In this introduction I intend to give a few helpful hints and tips that should make it easier for you to use this script to your best advantage. I'll also try to give some background to how this script has come to exist and why I made certain decisions through the writing process.

What is a Passion Play?

A passion play is simply a drama that details the last events of Jesus' life. Typically (as in this case), they cover the events from Palm Sunday to Easter Sunday. Originally a part of the mystery cycle, passion plays could be and were performed as stand-alone pieces of theatre. Like the rest of the cycle, they were written in the vernacular; they were rough, funny, moving, visual and extremely popular.

The most famous example of the form takes place every ten years at the German town of Oberammergau. The legend goes that the people of that town vowed to perform the play to thank God for being spared from the plague.

My script is simply called *The Passion Play*, but my hope is that whoever performs this play will rename it themselves. Traditionally, passion plays would take on the identity of the places where they were performed. For example, one of the first places this play was performed was Bradford, where they renamed it *The Bradford Passion*. Please feel free to do the same.

Why Do a Passion Play Today?

The story of the passion is fundamental to the Christian faith. It tells the story of how God loved the world enough to give His only son to die for us, to take the punishment for all of our wrongdoing and restore our relationship with God. Even as a narrative it is an incredibly moving and powerful story. If it is true, as I believe it is, it is a fantastic and world-changing account of love and forgiveness.

Yet in my work performing in schools and communities, I discovered that knowledge of the story can no longer be taken for granted, and that for those people who do know the bare facts of the story, too many dull assemblies and church services have dampened its impact. This seems tragic to me and I believe it is the duty of the church to tell people this story in a way that is dynamic and accessible.

If you've got to this point in the book then I hope that you already understand some of the wonderful qualities of the drama of the medieval church. Although, as we've seen, in the last thirty years or so theatre in the shape of professional Christian companies has again become part of the Christian landscape, drama within the church has remained largely at the level of the short sketch and does not rival the ambition or scope of the church of the Middle Ages.

A passion play could be a wonderful opportunity to bring churches together to attempt something ambitious and to communicate a story worth telling.

Language

If passion plays are so wonderful (you might argue) why bother with a new version? Why not simply stage the Easter sections of the York Mystery Cycle, for example?

My answer to that would be: you could certainly do that, and if you did I'd love to come and see it!

Unfortunately though, the English language has changed rather a lot since the mystery plays were first performed. Consequently, even in the volumes of the plays that are written with modern spelling, they can be extremely hard for a modern audience to understand.

For this reason I wanted to write my own modern version of the passion story, which would retain aspects of the style of the original but would be easier on the modern ear.

Style

As you will see, the play has been written in verse. This presents a number of challenges to actors, but it also has some really key advantages. Let's start with the advantages.

A simple rhythm gives a kind of energy to lines that comes across particularly well outside in street theatre settings. It makes the play easier to listen to and more dynamic. It has the effect of amplifying emotion and increasing tension as the narrative is put under the restrictive pressure of the metre and rhyme scheme. Have a look at the section below and you might be able to see what I mean.

Company: On us! On us! We take the blame!
Pilate: On you alone?
Company: We take the blame!
Pilate: You take the blame?
                 I grasp your offer.
                 Take him. Break him at Golgotha.
                 Stuff your hearts with vengeance full
                 At Calvary – place of the skull.

It also gave me the chance to create a few interesting effects in the writing process. For example, if the play is moving in a particular rhythm any line that is written with a different rhythm will be given a natural emphasis. Like this:

Jesus: The spirit is willing, the flesh is weak,
                 Fast asleep now, every one.
                 The spirit is willing, the flesh asleep
                 And see my betrayer, here he comes.

[Sure enough, a crowd of guards including Judas and Guards 1 and 2 are coming through the darkness with torches. They push through the audience as they start their lines.]

Guard 1:   How will we know which to grab?
                 Which man to capture, which to nab?
                 I would not be the mother's son
                 Who brings t'high priest the wrong one.
Guard 2:   A point well made Guard number one,
                 A point well made indeed,

> If we mistake this little task
> Them priests will make us bleed.
> Oh yes, I'll tell you this for starters
> Priests will have our guts for garters.

Here the slower rhythm and almost ritualistic rhyme scheme that Jesus employs (with the repetition of 'the spirit is willing, the flesh . . .') is contrasted with the faster, more colloquial lines of the Guards. This tells us something about the characters' attitudes to the events in which they are involved. Jesus is undertaking a great and terrible spiritual and physical ordeal but the Guards are simply doing their job, fearful of messing up and incurring the wrath of the High Priest.

The change in rhythm and tone also gives the audience's ears a break. If the same rhythm was used throughout it could easily become monotonous or hypnotic. The reason for changing tone is to keep the audience engaged and listening.

For a similar reason, at key points the rhyme scheme is abandoned all together. This lends an emphasis to important events in the story.

It's also worth noting that sometimes the rhyme is begun by one character and completed by a second, like this:

Peter: But you won't leave, my Lord and teacher, that can never be!

Jesus: I'm bound for death, my followers, to die upon a tree.

You may also notice that the language often has a northern flavour. Partly this has been done to honour the northern roots of the surviving mystery cycles, and I also chose to ground the story in an earthy regional dialect to emphasize the reality of what the disciples experienced.

A final advantage is that verse lines are easier to remember than prose.

However, the big disadvantage of verse is that if you aren't careful, the actors get so concerned with the rhythm of what they are saying that they might as well be saying 'te tum te tum te tum'. So the golden rule is that the verse is there to help you, but the acting comes first! Encourage your actors to play with the rhythm, but always go for sense and emotion over fitting in with the metre. It is there to serve you and not the other way around, so listen to it carefully and play with it, but don't let it control you.

Location

As is indicated in the script, the different scenes are intended to take place in different venues: some outside, some inside. The important thing is that you find the best possible locations that will work in your town for your audience.

It may be that you can't get access to lots of different places, or you think that for your audience a single easily controllable space would work best. Of course this is all right: whatever works for you.

However, the intention is that key scenes like the Palm Sunday section or the journey of Jesus to Calvary are performed as street theatre and that your actors then invite the audience to the other venues to follow the story.

The idea is that the audience gets a total experience. This is why I've suggested you actually serve a meal at The Last Supper so that the audience remembers the tastes and smells of the event. Essentially, my intention is that the experience be as vivid as possible.

Music

At various times in the script I've indicated that the company sings. I'm not a musician myself so I've just suggested lyrics which are direct quotations from Scripture. In most cases the moments are fairly brief so just a very simple melody should suffice. The purpose of these sections is to amplify the mood of the scene so if you don't have any skilled singers but do have an excellent guitarist, for example, please feel free to edit out the words and just provide music for these moments. If you wanted to use excerpts of existing worship songs please make sure you are aware of the relevant copyright issues.

Over to You . . .

As I hope I've made clear, this script is useless if it doesn't work for you. Please feel free to do whatever you need to do to get the best out of this play. I've loved writing it (though the decision to write it in verse came to haunt me: not much rhymes with Jesus!) and I really hope you have a great time producing it.

The Passion Play

This is a list of the speaking roles involved in this play. Many of these roles can be 'doubled', so in churches with fewer members the actors can play more than one role.

However, the play is deliberately ambitious in scope so my hope would be that, where possible, churches might join together to get a full cast and make this play as spectacular as possible.

[In order of appearance]

Chorus Leader
Peter
Mary Magdalene
Pharisee
Jesus
John
Judas
Andrew
Guard 1/Soldier 1
Guard 2/Soldier 2
Servant Girl

Man at Caiaphas' court
Caiaphas
Pontius Pilate
Barabbas
Simon of Cyrene
Man in crowd at crucifixion
Man 2
Sergeant
Thief 1
Thief 2
Mary, mother of Jesus
Joseph of Arimathea
Thomas
Philip

The Passion Play

Scene One – Palm Sunday

[The company process through the streets. They are Jesus' followers, his disciples and the women. They carry Jesus on their shoulders. The Chorus Leader beats a drum in time to the rhythm of their chanting. There is something of the Morris dance about them. Perhaps they could hand out flyers advertising the next parts of *The Passion Play*. They could also give party poppers and balloons to children. As the procession moves through the town they sing.]

Company: 'You will go out in joy
(sings)   And be led forth in peace;
                The mountains and the hills
                Will burst into song before you,
                And all the trees of the field
                Will clap their hands.'

[As the company reach the centre of town the song finishes and the leader takes up the new rhythm.]

Leader:	Who came from the heavens to banish the dark?
Company:	Jesus son of David did!
Leader:	Who tore the powers of Satan apart?
Company:	Jesus son of David did!
Leader:	Who made the blind see? Who healed the lame?
	Who scared the devil by the power of his name?
	Who saved us from the storm? And he'll save us again!
Company:	Jesus son of David did! Jesus son of David did!
Peter:	I met him in Galilee.
Company:	Jesus, Jesus, alleluia!
Peter:	He pulled the fish out of the sea!
Company:	Jesus, Jesus, alleluia!
Peter:	We said we'd follow him and then –
	He said he'd make us fish for men!
	We said it before and we'll say again!
Company:	Jesus, Jesus, alleluia! Jesus, Jesus, alleluia!
Mary:	He pulled demons out of me!
Company:	Jesus, Jesus, chosen one!
Mary:	Smashed the darkness, made me free!
Company:	Jesus, Jesus, chosen one!
Mary:	I was in the devil's lair.
	Seven demons held me there.
	He banished them, answered my prayer!
Company:	Jesus, Jesus, chosen one! Jesus, Jesus, chosen one!

[This can all repeat if required. Some of the company can be planted on the street to react to the passing procession. One of these should be the Pharisee, who now chooses his moment to heckle.]

Pharisee: Who does this man think he is?
Company: Jesus, Jesus, he's our king!
Pharisee: Jesus, stop them saying this!
Company: Jesus, Jesus, he's our king!
Pharisee: Stop them, Jesus, this is wrong!
They are saying you're God's son!
You're not the anointed one!
Company: Jesus, Jesus, he's our king! Jesus, Jesus,
he's our king!

[The rhythm stops and Jesus turns to look at the Pharisee.]

Jesus: I'll tell you true, if silence fell,
Then paving slabs and stones as well,
Would cry 'hosanna!' – shout my name.
Pharisee: I will never bawl the same!
This is blasphemy, obscene.
You'll regret what you have said.
You'll die within the week 'my king'
And crown of thorns will ring your
head.

[The rhythm crashes in again as the company answer the Pharisee.]

Company: Jesus, Jesus, he's our king! Jesus, Jesus,
he's our king! Jesus, Jesus, he's our
King! Jesus, Jesus, he's our king!

[The procession moves off, possibly to repeat this sequence in another part of the town, leaving the leader behind.]

Leader: So Jesus came to the city, and the
people called him king.
And they shouted praise with voices
raised,
And wasn't that a wondrous thing?
Yes, Jesus came to the city, and the
hypocrites were scared.
They created plans how to kill the man.
While the people cheered, the
priesthood glared,
The priesthood stared, the priesthood
stared.
While the people cheered all the priests
just glared.
They created plans how to kill the man,
While the people cheered . . . the
priesthood glared.

[The leader invites the crowd to the next venue.]

Scene Two – The Upper Room

[In a dark, small, warm room, perhaps lit by candles,
Jesus and his disciples are gathered together eating a
meal. The audience sit with them and the bread and
wine will be passed round them all. Ideally there is
enough food to actually give something to everyone
who comes. The idea of the scene is that it is an intimate,
private moment. To help with this perhaps the scene
could repeat a number of times, each time with just
a few audience members to share in it. This should be
a very special moment for company and audience
alike.]

Peter: I'll tell you lad, it seems quite clear
To me that I am held most dear,
And so you see I'm bragging not,
He called me Peter meaning 'rock'
And on that rock so Jesus claimed
He'd build a church to praise his name!

John: Aye, praise his name, not yours my son
And I'll be first when kingdom comes!

Jesus: My friends, my dearest brothers, see
What greatness is in Heaven's hall:
That I, your teacher, make myself the
servant of you all.
The first is last, the last is first, the
greatest shall be least
And I your teacher and your king –
shall wash your feet.

[Jesus gets a basin of water and offers to wash the feet of his disciples and all present.]

Peter: Hey, hang on, Lord! Don't touch my
feet. You're never washing me!

Jesus: But if I don't, no part of heaven's
kingdom can you be.

Peter: Then not my feet, but all of me feel free
to give a wash.

[Jesus washes Peter's feet.]

Jesus: I've washed your feet, and you are
clean,
For all but one, it is enough.

[Jesus moves round the group and gives them more food.]

Jesus: I've looked forward to this meal
                    With you my dearest friends, although
                    One of you eating with me here will
                        turn on me,
                    And this is how you'll know
                    The traitor, he's the one I give this
                        bread I dip.

[He dips a piece of bread and gives it to Judas.]

Judas: Me a traitor? Is it me?
Jesus: Well, you said it.

[Judas pushes his way out and exits. Jesus goes to the bread and lifts it up and breaks it.]

Jesus: This is my body; broken for you, do
                        this in memory of me.
Andrew: [to Peter] In memory? Is that what he
                        said?

[Jesus pours the wine.]

Jesus: This is my blood poured out for you,
                        do this in memory of me.

[They share the wine.]

Jesus: As often as you eat this meal together,
                        please remember.
Peter: But you won't leave, my Lord and
                        teacher, that can never be!

Jesus: I'm bound for death, my followers, to
             die upon a tree.
             And though my body shakes in fear,
             Though my heart beats faster still,
             Though my sweat and though my tears
             Revolt I'll do my father's will.
             It seems good, to God my father,
             That I'm given up to die.
             To the four winds you'll be scattered,
             And my name you will deny.

Peter: Aye, some of these are flaky sorts,
             Feckless, fickle, fleeing fast.
             But I am not so cheaply bought
             And I'll still be there at the last.

Jesus: Simon Peter, you will run
             And say you never knew my name,
             Before the cock crows morning come,
             Disown me once then twice again.

Peter: I won't, I bloody won't!

Jesus: We'll see.

Peter: Aye, you will see I bloody won't!

Jesus: What must be will be. But don't
             Think I condemn you. Come with me,
             My friends and brothers. Quiet and
                prayerful
             For a time now, I would be.
             If you would comfort me a little,
             Meet me at Gethsemane.

[Jesus leaves and one by one his disciples follow until
only Peter and Andrew are left.]

Andrew: And might I ask . . . ?
Peter: Don't ask me! I've got no clue!

Andrew:	Does he sound like a king to you?
	I've never met a monarch yet
	Who spoke so much of his own death!
Peter:	But you've seen all that he's performed.
	And I've heard when he first was born,
	Angelic hosts surrounded him.
	So don't ask me if he's a king.
	No other monarch I can see
	Lays claim to greater sovereignty.
Andrew:	Well, true or not, it does appear
	That we are on our own in here.
	We've dawdled chatting, now we find
	That you and I are left behind.
Peter:	Let's go! Let's go! Let's not be late!
	And to Gethsemane make haste!

[They hurry off.]

Scene Three – Gethsemane

[Again the scene changes location. Naturally, the garden is an outdoor location and it is evening. Take care that the scene is well lit, but without destroying the quiet atmosphere that comes with dusk.]

Company:	'The Lord's my shepherd, I'll
[sings]	not want, he makes me lie down in
	green pastures.'
Jesus:	My heart is full of anguish, sorrow.
	My eyes, they burn with fiery tears.
	Stay here awhile and pray I beg you.
	I won't give way to my fears.

[As Jesus moves away from his disciples they, one by one, fall asleep.]

Jesus: Father, you can do all things, you
                    framed the canvas of the skies
                Ignited stars and forged the mountain
                    that beneath them lies.
                You threw, in fury flung the fiery orb,
                    the sun, and guide his rays
                You rested when your work was done,
                    to you, your son kneels – to you he
                    prays.

[Jesus falls to his knees and, in desperation, prays.]

Jesus: Let this cup of sorrow pass from me.
                Take this dread responsibility.
                Find some other sacrifice
                To settle Adam's price,
                Not me. Not me. Not me. Not me.

[Jesus wipes away his tears and sweat as he comes to
a fresh resolution.]

Jesus: But I will do your will, my Father.
                I won't falter from your call.
                If no other pathway's found,
                Then I will pay for Adam's fall.
                Every punishment is mine now,
                I will pay for everything,
                For the love of Adam's race,
                The Lamb of God will become sin.

[Jesus slowly stands and returns to the disciples. He finds them fast asleep.]

Jesus: The spirit is willing, the flesh is weak,
                    Fast asleep now, every one.
                    The spirit is willing, the flesh asleep.
                    And see my betrayer, here he comes.

[Sure enough, a crowd of guards including Judas and Guards 1 and 2 are coming through the darkness with torches. They push through the audience as they start their lines.]

Guard 1:   How will we know which to grab?
                    Which man to capture, which to nab?
                    I would not be the mother's son
                    Who brings t'high priest the wrong one.
Guard 2:   A point well made, Guard number one,
                    A point well made indeed.
                    If we mistake this little task
                    Them priests will make us bleed.
                    Oh yes, I'll tell you this for starters
                    Priests will have our guts for garters.
Guard 1:   Guts for garters?
Guard 2:   Guts for garters!
Both: Priests'll have our guts for garters.
Guard 1:   A point well made Guard number two
                    A thing most rightly said.
                    If we mistake or mess this up
                    Them priests'll have our heads.
                    Oh, if we take the wrong man hence
                    Our lives are not worth fifty pence.
Guard 2:   Not fifty pence?
Guard 1:   Not fifty pence!
Both: Our lives are not worth fifty pence!

Judas: Shut up! The both of you shut up!
                    And listen up to this:
                    You won't mistake or mess this up
                    Just grab the man you see me kiss.

[Judas approaches Jesus.]

Judas: Teacher!

[Judas kisses Jesus.]

Jesus: With a kiss, you betray the Son of
                    Man.

[The guards go to grab him. Jesus turns to the crowd.]

Jesus: And you, each day you know I taught
                    The people in the temple court.
                    Why could you not arrest me then?
                    Instead you come now with armed men,
                    As if I were some freedom fighter,
                    Take my hands and bind them tighter.
                    I'm the same man I have been,
                    I'm the same man all have seen
                    Make clean the sinner, heal the lame,
                    Make the blind man see again,
                    And now you come with club and knife
                    To try me, kill me, take my life!
                    . . . But it is written,
                    Blood must be spilled,
                    For Heaven's word to be fulfilled . . .
                    For Heaven's word to be fulfilled
                    Blood must be shed, I must be killed.

[They bind his hands.]

Jesus:	These, my disciples, let them go
	And I'll along with you.
Judas:	You'll come with us without such terms,
	Come where we want you to.
Guard 1:	Nay, let the others move along
	I've had no orders touching them.
	I'll not overstep the priest's command,
	Unhand the others, men!

[The guards unhand the disciples, who run off, and then they carry Jesus away.]

Scene Four –
Jesus' Trial and Peter's Denial

[Outside Caiaphas' house, in the courtyard. We can see lights on inside the house and possibly see Jesus with his back to the window facing his accusers, but we can't hear what is being said. Instead we stay outside with the priest's servants and Peter.]

Peter:	Jesus wouldn't let me fight them,
	So I followed here,
	Waiting in the dark and frightened,
	Shuddering with fear.
	Judas came and hand-delivered,
	Former friend so cheaply sold,
	Then he left but I'm still waiting
	In the dark and cold, so cold,
	In the dark and cold.

[He tries to see or hear what's happening but he can't, so he turns to the nearest servant girl.]

Peter: Can you hear what's being said?
          I can hardly see at all.
          What's taking so long in there?
          What's going on inside that hall?
          I'm so sick of standing waiting
          For somebody to appear.
          Don't they know the man's done
              nothing?
          What's Jesus got to fear?

Servant Girl: What to fear? What has he not!
          That's Caiaphas – the dread high priest.
          That Jesus won't escape from there,
          Without a flogging at the least.
          No heretic or gross blasphemer
          Will escape the High Priest's sight
          Before he's lost at least some blood
          And lucky not to lose his life.

Peter: He hasn't got the power to kill,
          That's Pilate's right and precedent!

Servant Girl: But who's to stop them beating him
              to death
          And call it 'accident'?

[Whispers come back from nearer the door.]

Man: They're asking Jesus loads of questions
          Giving him the third degree.
          They've brought in all these witnesses,
          But their statements don't agree.
          One says Jesus did a thing,
          The other swears that he did not.
          God help this fellow if the verdict
          Hangs on the testimony of this lot!

Peter:	And Jesus? How's he answering?
	How does he refute their claims?
Man:	In truth he's saying not a word,
	But silently he takes their blame.
	And silently he stands in chains.
	He hangs his head and stands alone,
	Apparently ashamed.

[Peter shakes his head, confused. He notices the Servant Girl is staring at him.]

Peter:	What do you think you're looking at?
	Don't you know it's rude to stare?
Servant Girl:	I know you, don't I?
	You were with the fellow who's in there!
Peter:	Like heck I was!
	And you should keep a closer watch upon your tongue!
Servant Girl:	You sound like one of his as well!
	But perhaps I've got it wrong.
Peter:	Perhaps you have! Perhaps you have!
	And you should get your facts straight first.
	This freezing trial is bad enough without your tongue
	To make bad worse!
Man:	Now they've asked him most directly if he is the chosen one,
	If he's come from most High God, if he is His son.
	Jesus looks straight forward now and calmly makes his stand,
	Softly, almost whispering, he says 'You rightly say I am'.

Peter: Oh, what's he saying? What's he saying?
                     Playing right into their hands,
                     That's just what they wanted from him,
                     Using God's own name 'I AM'!
                     Each Pharisee and true believer
                     Will denounce him as blasphemer,
                     Claiming his own parity
                     With spotless pure divinity.
                     Oh if I'd thought he'd freely choose
                     To put his own neck in the noose,
                     I would not a moment lose before
                     I tried to set him free.

Man: But what does this man mean to you?
                     That you're so angry, so confused?
                     You fellows must indeed be close
                     To jeopardize your liberty!

Peter: Why don't you make your accusation?
                     I'm sick of insinuation
                     And resent your defamation
                     That I ever knew this man!
                     Jesus is to me unknown,
                     Now get you gone, leave me alone!

Servant Girl: And yet you can get so upset.
                     I've never known a fellow yet
                     That shouts and roars and tears his hair
                     For one he's never met!

Peter: I don't, I don't, I've never known him!
                     I repeat it's not a lie!

[The cock crows. At this moment, Peter realizes what he's said and sinks to his knees.]

Peter: Three times, just like he said, three
                          times
                     I have his name denied.

[Peter weeps. The door to the high priest's house opens and Caiaphas emerges.]

Caiaphas: Blasphemy! We all have heard it!
Curse this man! He has deserved it!
Take him off to Pontius Pilate
There a further trial he'll face.
All of you along with us,
To seek that justice from above,
That we have earned through loyal love
Come now to Pilate's place!

[Jesus is driven through the audience, the guards and the priests start to follow. Judas enters.]

Judas: Wait, Caiaphas!
I beg you wait,
I've made mistakes. I wouldn't see
A guiltless man brought to the stake,
Here, now reclaim your fee.

[He throws his purse of money down.]

Judas: The devil led me far astray
This noble Jesus to betray.
Please take your money back I pray,
And set this fellow free.

Caiaphas: Thanks for the cash Iscariot,
Sadly, you're too late. I'll not
Prevent the wheels of justice turning,
Here, take again your hard-won
    earnings.
Don't be ashamed – the man is guilty.

Judas: I won't touch that tainted money.
Take it, leave it, let it lie.
I am going off to die,
A rope will usher me to hell.
My death be on your head as well.

[Judas runs off.]

Caiaphas: Guiltless of both as God's my witness.
But I must to other business,
Pontius Pilate now awaits,
On his decision hangs our fate.

[Caiaphas leaves. Peter is alone.]

Peter: Forgive me, God, a wretched man.
I'm anguished, sobbing, sorrowful,
So wracked with guilt I scarcely see
How I'll go on at all.
That blameless man, that guiltless lamb,
Innocent, most in need of friends,
And I, his rock, so fast deny I even
   know him
At the end.
I won't see Roman Procurator
Listen to those bloody traitors,
I won't see my sweet Lord die,
I'll lie low instead, and hide.

[Peter goes off in the opposite direction.]

Scene Five – Pilate's Court

[Again, this is a big public scene that could easily take place either in the street or in an enclosed venue. It starts with Jesus being pushed on. Pilate stands.]

Pilate: You stand before the voice of Rome,
                  Mouthpiece of imperial might.
                  What beaten cur, what dog is this
                  You drag before my sight?

Caiaphas: This man is Jesus called by name,
                  A radical whose growing fame
                  Will soon unseat your power here
                  Unless perchance he 'disappears'.
                  He's broken laws, promoted sin,
                  He's called himself the Jewish king.

Pilate: It seems that I should speak with him,
                  See if these charges hold.
                  Jesus, king of all the Jews,
                  Tell me are these stories true?
                  Should Rome's official bow to you?
                  Or are these lies I'm told?

Jesus: It is as you say.

Pilate: That's all you say, your final word?
                  These grievous charges I have heard
                  Surely require a full reply.

Caiaphas: He's said enough, now let him die.

Pilate: Now let him die? That's your request?
                  I've seen nothing to suggest
                  A flogging will not sate your rage.

[Jesus is taken away and whipped.]

Caiaphas: No, we would have him die, my liege.

Pilate: Oh, would you see him die?

Caiaphas:	We would.
	And it is politic you should
	Give ear to us, the people cry.
Company:	Yes, yes, crucify!
Pilate:	But tell me now: what is his sin?
Company:	Crucify him! Crucify him!
Pilate:	So you will not be denied.
Company:	No! We'll see him crucified!
Pilate:	Listen now to what I say,
	What would you think to a trade?
	To mark this festival I will
	Release a man who should be killed.
	Bring out the prisoners.

[Jesus and Barabbas are brought out.]

Pilate:	One of these must die today
	But which one, that's the tricky thing,
	Barabbas: murderer, and killer
	Or Jesus: teacher, healer, king?
Company:	Barabbas! Barabbas!
Pilate:	Barabbas? Now, are you sure?
	You would free a terrorist,
	Who's killed his share of men and more?
	What factors sway your choice in this?
Company:	Barabbas! Barabbas!
Pilate:	And what about the Jewish king?
Company:	Crucify him! Crucify him!
Pilate:	Isn't that a curious thing?
	You would sooner free a killer,
	Free a man who drips with blood,
	Than spare a harmless lunatic
	Who thinks he does the will of God.
Company:	Crucify him! Crucify him!

[Pilate calls for a basin of water and washes his hands during this next speech.]

Pilate:	Crucify him? Witness this:
	I wash my hands free of this business,
	Of his blood I am guiltless!
Company:	On us! On us! We take the blame!
Pilate:	On you alone?
Company:	We take the blame!
Pilate:	You take the blame?
	I grasp your offer.
	Take him. Break him at Golgotha.
	Stuff your hearts with vengeance full
	At Calvary – place of the skull.
Company:	Crucify him! Crucify him! Crucify him!
	Crucify him!

[They grab Jesus and put a crown of thorns on his head. Then they make him carry his cross through the street. Jesus has been badly beaten and struggles to carry it.]

Soldier 1:	Hurry up now, regal one!
	We haven't got all day.
Soldier 2:	We don't get overtime, my son.
	Let's move along the way.
Soldier 1:	Get your shoulder under it!
	Come on now, don't you shirk.
Soldier 2:	Look at him, underfed, unfit,
	No good for proper work.

[Jesus collapses in the street.]

Soldier 1:	I swear, he'll never make the walk
	He can't even stand!

[Soldier 2 sees Simon of Cyrene in the crowd.]

Soldier 2:   Hey you! Don't just stand and gawp
Come on now, lend a hand!

[Simon helps Jesus to carry the cross to Golgotha. It is probably best if this is an indoor venue, so that you can more easily control the conditions.]

Scene Six – Golgotha

[At Golgotha, two Thieves have already been crucified. As the audience come in they hang on their crosses. The crowd surge in shouting. Jesus is near collapse, and indeed falls to the ground as soon as they reach the right spot.]

Company: Crucify him! Crucify him!

[Simon kneels beside where Jesus has fallen.]

Simon of   I've brought your burden to this place,
Cyrene: But you must do the rest, I fear.
God bless you, friend, and help you
    face
The torment that awaits you here.

[He pushes his way out through the crowd and the Soldiers stretch Jesus out on the cross. He is crucified, and the Soldiers gamble for his clothes.]

Man: He saved others didn't he?
Why can't he save himself then, too?
Man 2:   What's that sign above his head?

Man:	It states he is king of the Jews.
Man 2:	Does that not presume too much?
	It should say 'This is what he claimed'.
Sergeant:	It's me who put that placard up
	And what I've written will remain!
Soldier 1:	Three sixes! Ha! I win his coat.
Soldier 2:	His coat's all smeared and stiff with blood!
	It's ruined, useless, so is his cloak!
Soldier 1:	I've got his shirt too!
Soldier 2:	It's no good!
	There's gashes where the whip's gone through,
	It's lousy, bloody, torn to shreds.
	That rag's a worthless thing to you,
	It's sopping with the blood he's shed.
Soldier 1:	You played and lost, my sorry mate.
	It's funny now that you have lost,
	The goods seem worthless. Sour grapes,
	I say to you, you wine-soaked sot!
Soldier 2:	Wine-soaked what? I'll have your head!
	I'll have your head upon my spear!
Soldier 1:	Why, come on then, you drunken get!
	See what reception you get here!
	Come on, you think you are so fierce,
	Come try your luck with me, my son.
	I'll stick you ere my ribs are pierced
	And you'll be dead before I'm done.
Sergeant:	If either blockhead stirs a foot,
	I'll run you both through with my sword.
	Sit down, and both of you shut up
	And don't you say another word!
Jesus:	Father, forgive them. They don't know what they do.

Caiaphas: You saved others! But who'll save you?

[Mary, mother of Jesus, has been standing nearby and can finally stand it no longer.]

Mary: Stop! Please stop! This is my son!

[Jesus looks around.]

Jesus: Where's John? Where's John?

[John pushes his way through the crowd.]

John: I'm here, my Lord.
Jesus: Then hear my word.
                  You see my mum?
                  Take her, John, as your own mother,
                  Give her shelter. Mother, see
                  John standing here, this is your son,
                  Please comfort him as you would me.

[John and Mary try to comfort one another, and for a moment there's quiet. Then one of the Thieves stirs himself and taunts Jesus.]

Thief 1:   Jesus, come, king of the Jews,
                  Don't another moment lose!
                  But get yourself down from this tree,
                  And while you're at it, set me free!
                  Hurry up, your majesty!
                  You won't last long now – here comes
                      death!
                  Employ that sweet divinity
                  I've heard that you possess!
                  Shall I tell you all the facts?

Your lungs are starting to collapse,
Each burning, painful exhalation
Brings you closer to damnation,
And as you feel your breathing fail,
You lift yourself up by the nails
To try to get a breath of air,
And skin and ripping sinew tears,
And that's the last sound you will hear.
You'll die, suffocating here.

[Jesus stays silent. Thief 2 has noticed what has been going on and shouts his response.]

Thief 2:   Don't you even fear your maker?
Soon you'll meet with your creator
What will you say to Him then?
That scorn and hatred marked your
          end?
It's right and just that we should die,
We're thieves and killers, you and I,
But this man here is not to blame.
He's done no wrong. I know his name,
And long heard others talk of him,
I've heard no hint of any sin.
It's not right he should die like this,
They have no right to mark his flesh,
No nails should touch his feet and
          hands,
Nor dogs like you abuse the man,
No games of dice played at his feet,
No crowd of jeering mockers speak.
When each man dies, he dies alone.
Remember me, Lord, on your throne.
No one remembered truly dies –

Jesus: This day you'll be in paradise.
Your eyes my father's home will see
You'll see, you'll see, you'll see . . .

[Jesus is in a kind of delirium from the pain and suddenly roars out to the heavens:]

Jesus: *Eloi, Eloi, lama Sabachthane!*
My God, my God, why have you
forsaken me?

Caiaphas: Oh, won't your father save your life?
Oh Son of Man! Oh chosen one!
Come now, you say you are the Christ,
Why won't your Father save His son?
Could it be you were mistaken?
I have to ask your pardon, sire,
Does your sudden killing match your
expectation,
My Messiah?
I know you mentioned martyrdom,
But, you see, I must confess
That I assumed 'anointed ones'
Met endings far more glorious!

[The lights go out, and there is darkness.]

Sergeant: Be silent, priest, can you not tell
Some power is working here?
Whether of heaven or of hell,
There's something more to this, I fear.

Jesus: Father, into your hands I commit my
spirit.

Sergeant: I'm sorry, lad, you're not due death for
hours yet, maybe for days.

	After a while we'll break your legs to
	speed you on your way.
	That will help, I promise you. I won't
	leave you hanging long.
Jesus:	It is finished! It is finished!

[He is dead. Thunder rattles the sky and the ground seems to shake.]

Sergeant:	Surely this man was God's son.
Caiaphas:	Make sure of him now.
	Pierce his side and through his chest
	Stab his heart within his breast.
Sergeant:	Do what he says, lads, do your best,
	And leave him hanging in this place.
	Then guard his carcass till Pilate
	Says where his corpse shall rest.

[The soldiers stab Jesus. The soldiers and the priests and most of the company leave. Joseph of Arimathea approaches, looks up at Jesus for a moment, then turns to the audience.]

Joseph:	My name is Joseph of Arimathea,
	Afraid to speak for him before.
	But in His death I'll give him shelter,
	Entomb the King I did adore.
	Come my friends and take him down,
	And with respect and reverent fear,
	Anoint his body, remove the crown
	And bear his corpse away from here.

[Mary Magdalene and Mary, mother of Jesus, help Joseph take the body down. They carry him out slowly, softly singing 'Man of sorrows acquainted with grief'.]

Scene Seven – The Upper Room

[The audience are crowded into a small room. The door is locked after they come in. The disciples are gathered together, deeply depressed and traumatized by what's happened to them.]

Andrew: It's been three days now since his death.
We've barely moved. We've hardly left
This room at all. What's next? What's
next?

Peter: We're hunted now. You count on this,
That Caiaphas won't let us live.
He will not rest. He will not give
Quarter to us few that remain.

Thomas: Yes, count on it; he'll hunt us down.
He won't quit cos we've gone to
ground.
Nor rest until each one is found
And in his grasp again.

Philip: I can't believe it's come to this,
Delivered by a traitor's kiss,
A man who we were brothers with.
Jesus himself selected him.

Peter: Judas is dead.

Andrew: I didn't know.

Philip: He put a noose around his throat.
And hanged his body from a rope
As payment for his sin.

Peter: A pointless, worthless suicide,
A wretched traitor dog he died,
Unmourned, unburied let him lie
And let his hide decay.

Thomas:	He'll surely face the fire of God.
	They found him in the field of blood.
	His guts had burst, and like a dog
	The devil took his soul away.
Andrew:	And now like dogs they hunt for us
	And who knows who is treacherous?
	And who knows who is weak enough
	To take the rope as well?
	Though Judas was the weakest here,
	The second weakest may appear
	His life to take, and I do fear
	To join Judas in hell!
Philip:	Don't talk like that!
Andrew:	Why shouldn't I?
	We let him down! We let him die!
	We fled like children from his side!
Thomas:	We had no choice, Andrew!
Peter:	We had no choice? What lame excuse
	Is that? We fled at time of truth,
	Abandoned him! No earthly use
	Was I to him, nor you!
Thomas:	And if we'd stayed we would have died,
	Each one of us been crucified.
	Would that make you more satisfied,
	For you to feel his pain?
Peter:	I don't know, but I swear to you,
	I'd give a lot just to undo
	The time when I swore words untrue
	And disavowed his name.
Philip:	This talking gets us nowhere fast,
	Confuses us, we miss our way.
	This raking over what is past
	Is useless. Let's just sit and pray.

[They sit in silence for a time. Suddenly there's a knock at the door. The boys grab weapons.]

Peter: Tool up, they've come!
Thomas: Take up your blades.
We'll make them pay a price most dear.
Philip: We'll make them run,
Don't be afraid!
Andrew: We'll make them pay to come in here!

[Peter looks through a gap in the door.]

Peter: It's all right. Stand down.
Don't fear or fret.
It's Mary on the other side.
Andrew: Why'd she have to knock like that?
I was flippin' terrified!

[Peter opens the door and Mary Magdalene and the other women come in.]

Mary: Listen to me, I have news.
Listen please, please gather round.
I and the other women sprinted to the tomb,
And there we found the body gone,
The stone rolled away,
The ground was bare. The grave clothes lay
Folded where he had been bound
But why and how I couldn't say . . .
Thomas: Who's taken him, who's stolen him?
Who would do this grievous thing?
Who would sin – to desecrate
Our sweet Lord's final resting place?

Mary: I looked within the grave, and through
                   The tears that blurred my sight,
                   Two men, or so it seemed to me,
                   Two men I saw, but made of light.
                   And they whispered to me then:
                   'Woman, say why do you weep?'
                   For I did weep with ceaseless pain,
                   Choking as I tried to speak.
                   I said 'My master's disappeared,
                   I don't know why, or where to seek.'
                   And then, in truth I don't know why,
                   I turned around and there I found
                   A single man standing close by.
                   The gardener, so I assumed,
                   And asked him straight 'If you've
                     removed
                   My Lord from me,
                   Please won't you state where he can be?
                   Please won't you say?
                   So I can go to be with him
                   And take my Lord away.'
                   'Mary,' he said. Then I saw
                   The man more clearly than before,
                   Like scales had fallen from my eyes,
                   Cascaded with the tears I cried.
                   'Rabboni! Teacher!' I proclaimed,
                   Gasping, shocked as I exclaimed.
                   For it was Jesus, standing there,
                   And tears of joy now streaked my face,
                   That he had come in my despair
                   And found me in that place.
                   And then he bade me come to you
                   And tell you plainly what I've learned,
                   That you'd rejoice at what is true
                   Our Jesus has returned!

Peter:	Mary, please, I beg you stop.
	Madness grips you. Hold your tongue.
	We saw him die upon the cross,
	We saw him die, and he is gone.
Mary:	But it is true. I wouldn't lie,
	Nor does my grief my mind deceive.
Thomas:	Unless I see with my own eyes,
	Then I will not believe.
Philip:	Nor I.
Andrew:	Nor I.
Peter:	Nor none of us.
	Each one must bear our master's loss.
	We saw him broken on that cross.
Mary:	But what I've said is true!
Andrew:	I know you thought, I know you said.
	He was God's son but his wounds bled
	Just like a normal man's instead.
Jesus:	Peace be with each of you.

[This is obviously a tricky moment to make Jesus suddenly appear. Possibly he could have entered with Mary, concealed amongst the women. Alternatively, pretend to lock the door behind Mary after she comes in so Jesus appears to enter through a locked door. Other solutions depend on the room you're in but he could also be hidden somewhere. If you select this option, though, it is imperative that your actor can't be accidentally discovered as the sight of 'Jesus' crouching in a cupboard might rather undermine the suspension of disbelief!]

Jesus:	Don't be afraid. Don't be alarmed.
	What Mary told you is the truth.
	Thomas, how is your faith now
	You see me stand as living proof?

Thomas: Forgive me, Lord, I do believe,
              But yet I know eyes can deceive.

Jesus: Take my hand, set your heart at ease,
              I am no ghost you see.

Thomas: I see, I truly see indeed.
              I saw you die, I saw you bleed
              But here you stand. You live and
                  breathe.
              You have returned to me.

Jesus: To you, and to you all as well.
              I've broken sin, I've ransacked hell,
              In heaven's favour all may dwell
              Who call upon my name.
              All human sin I took on me
              Upon that cross at Calvary,
              And my death paid the penalty
              For all sin – you may live unstained
              And in God's favour all may live,
              Your daily sins he will forgive.
              I came for all, new life to give,
              To cleanse the sinner, dry his tears.
              But here I can't remain for long.
              Don't be afraid when I am gone,
              Wait and you'll see my spirit come
              To be your guide, and help you here.
              Satan's power it is defeated,
              Come now raise your voice!
              My task on earth it is completed
              With the angels now rejoice!

[The company sing.]

Emma's Mystery: An Introduction

Emma's Mystery is particularly dear to my heart because
it is the first play I wrote that was ever professionally
performed. I remember writing the first draft over a
Christmas holiday and then rewriting it for about a
year. Saltmine Theatre Company first performed it,
touring it around the country as well as taking it to
the Edinburgh Festival Fringe and the 2006 Keswick
Convention.

The Concept

The concept of the play is fairly straightforward. Emma
is a teenager going through a difficult time in her life.
Her father died two years ago and her mother has
started to see another man. In an attempt to cope, Emma
has thrown herself into her schoolwork and, as the play
starts, is revising for a Religious Education examination
that focuses on the life of Christ. She falls asleep at her
desk and starts to dream the events of the gospel . . .

As a writer, this set-up allowed me the opportunity
to let biblical characters interact with the modern world

in an interesting way. Since the audience are never sure if what they are seeing is really happening or all just part of a dream that Emma is having, they are free to enjoy surreal moments, odd grotesque characters and curious juxtapositions between the biblical events and the modern surroundings without thinking 'This would never happen'. In a dream, anything can happen. So, for example, in the scene set in the temple courtyard the books on Emma's desk are brought to life by the actors, to become pigeons being sold for people to sacrifice.

Style

The style of the play has been greatly influenced by what is known as Physical Theatre. This is a kind of performance that is non-naturalistic and relies upon the bodies of the actors and the imaginations of the audience to bring the play to life.

It calls for a kind of suppleness of both body and mind from the performers, who often have to change rapidly from one character to the next. Saltmine performed the play with four actors. One actor played Emma, another played Jesus and one of the Pharisees, and the other two played everybody else, altering their posture and voices to signal the changes.

Scenes

To help make this play as user-friendly as possible, I've split it up into ten scenes of different lengths. However, when Saltmine performed the play it was not divided up and the scenes simply flowed into one another. I'd recommend that you try to preserve that same smooth flowing quality even though there are now separate scenes marked in.

Masks

The idea to put the Pharisees in masks came from a desire to make them as terrifying as possible. They were played not as people at all but as something else – animals or demons, perhaps. The movements developed by the actors to play these characters reflected this.

My wife made the masks from papier-mâché, based on some masks we found that were used in Japanese Noh theatre. We took the hair for them from a Santa Claus beard we found in a costume shop! These worked well and there's no reason why you couldn't do something similar.

There are many different schools of thought surrounding performance in masks, but this is how Saltmine created these Pharisee characters. We held the masks in our hands and looked at them as though they were our own faces, and tried to breathe as the mask might. Then we put the masks on and looked into a mirror at our masked reflections. We attempted to 'complete the mask' with the bottom half of our faces – the unmasked mouth and chin – so that the whole face appeared to be part of the mask. This took a little while as we experimented with how to move our mouths and chins so that they looked and felt as though they belonged to the mask.

Once we were happy with the faces, we worked down through the neck, the shoulders and the rest of the body until we had created the physicality of the mask character. Finally we began to experiment with different voices for these characters and only after much work,

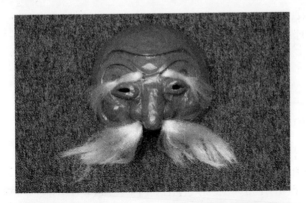

Pharisee 1

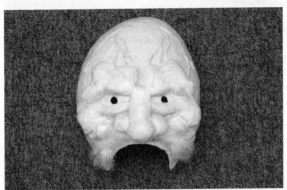

Pharisee 2

Pharisee 3

Photo courtesy of James White at Saltmine Media

trial and error did we try to get these mask creatures to say lines of the script.

The key to it, I think, is to have fun and not to worry if it seems childish or silly at first. Keep playing until you find something that works for you.

Music

Music is an excellent tool for quickly establishing mood and atmosphere, which in a play as fast-moving as this is a definite plus. When Saltmine performed it we used Gregorian chants for the scenes with the Pharisees, and African American spirituals for some of the other scenes. However, when the cast changed the new actor playing Jesus was also an accomplished musician, so we incorporated some of his music as well.

One song that I would recommend using is the 'Coventry Carol'. This is a surviving fragment from an otherwise lost mystery cycle, and it is a beautiful song. It tells the story of the death of the innocents at the hands of Herod and, as you'll see in the script, we sang it for the two series of tableaux representing Jesus' nativity and crucifixion. It seems to me to capture at once the beauty and the sadness of much of Jesus' life. Also, as the one link to the original mystery cycle, it was an important inclusion for me.

Part of the physical theatre style is that the actors create everything themselves and the audience's imagination fills any gaps. Consequently we tried to create all the music ourselves rather than relying on recorded tracks (we did slightly compromise on this eventually and had a recorded guitar track for some of the later performances). This worked well and I think an audience likes the feeling that the whole performance is live and being created 'just for them'. I would recommend that you try to do something similar yourselves. As ever though, use the gifts that you've been given: if you have a wonderful percussionist or violinist or oboe player or . . . well, you get the idea.

Audience Response

In my experience, audiences have really loved *Emma's Mystery*. They seem to respond particularly strongly to the innocence and the naiveté that comes from seeing the story through the eyes of someone not yet fully adult.

Interestingly, though, a number of people that I spoke to rather misinterpreted this as meaning that the play must be aimed at children or young people. Although I would be delighted if those groups enjoyed the play, it was never my intention that they would be the main audience for it. It was and is intended as a play for adults that just happens to have a teenager as the central character.

I hope that you enjoy reading this play and I would be delighted to learn that people were performing it again. God bless you all and best wishes.

Emma's Mystery

Character List

[In order of appearance]

Emma
Linda (Emma's mother)
Richard (Linda's boyfriend)
Mary, mother of Jesus
Joseph
John the Baptist
Jesus
Satan
Abel
Pharisee 1
Pharisee 2
Pharisee 3
Mary Magdalene
Disciple 1
Disciple 2
Teacher of the Law
Mary, sister of Martha
Lazarus
Temple Traders

Scene One

[As the lights come up we discover Emma sitting at a table, books in front of her, her head resting on the table. The set of the play is extremely simple. There is a table and a chair and a large wardrobe or cupboard at the back of the stage. Other than that the stage is bare. Moments pass before Emma looks up wearily and picks up the Bible.]

Emma: 'In the beginning was the Word, and the
(reading) Word was with God, and the Word was God. He was with God in the beginning. Through him all things were made; without him nothing was made that has been made. In him was life, and that life was the light of men. The light shines in the darkness, but the darkness has not understood it.' I don't understand it.

[She sits in frustrated silence. Gradually we hear voices off. Emma groans and wearily lifts her head.]

Richard [off]: Will anyone be in?
Linda [off]: I think Emma's working on something; she has an exam coming up.
Richard [off]: Oh.

[Richard and Linda enter, removing their coats and hanging them on the coat-stand.]

Linda: Tea?
Emma: No thanks.
Linda: Richard?

Richard:	Please. Two su–
Linda:	Two sugars. I remember.

[They smile at this. Linda exits to make the tea. Richard and Emma are left rather awkwardly alone.]

Richard:	So how are you Emma?
Emma:	Fine, thanks.

[Richard walks over to the books beside Emma and begins flicking through them.]

Richard:	What are you reading? *The Life of Christ*, *Man or God?*, *The Holy Bible*. Physics, right?
Emma:	No.
Richard:	No, no. It was just a joke
Emma:	Thanks for telling me.
Richard:	Not at all. Can I help?
Emma:	Not unless you can somehow make 'the life of Christ' more interesting to me than whatever's on TV.
Richard:	Let's see: 'Many have undertaken to draw up an account of the things that have been fulfilled among us, just as they were handed down to us by those who from the first were eyewitnesses.' Yes. Sorry, I don't think so, actually.

[Enter Linda with the tea.]

Linda:	There you are, love.
Richard:	Thanks.

[Linda watches as Richard drinks a bit.]

Linda:	Is it all right?
Richard:	It's perfect, thank you.
Linda:	Well, look at that. I've forgotten my tea after all that!

[Richard laughs. Linda exits. Emma has been watching this with barely concealed irritation.]

Emma:	She's such an idiot sometimes.
Richard:	Emma, she's your mother.
Emma:	So?
Richard:	Well, you shouldn't be . . . you know . . .
Emma:	Richard, what are you doing here anyway?
Richard:	Sorry?
Emma:	What are you doing here? I mean, this isn't your home.
Richard:	Well . . . I know it isn't, but . . .
Emma:	You don't live here.
Richard:	I know I don't . . .

[He is interrupted by the return of Linda with her cup of tea.]

Linda:	Ah, that's better. Now, have you told Emma about the party?
Emma:	What party?
Richard:	Well, no, I was just about to say. Well, um, yes, well, it isn't a party really. Just a few friends, we're meeting up at my place to watch the comet, apparently you'll be able to see it really clearly tonight. I've got a

	telescope set up and, well, that's it really. You're both welcome.
Emma:	Is anyone else sick of this comet? You can't turn the telly on without seeing it.
Linda:	Well, Richard was telling me that it's pretty amazing that we're getting to see it at all, it hasn't been seen in – Is it a thousand years, Richard?
Richard:	No, no, two thousand I think they said.
Emma:	Honestly, do I look interested?
Linda:	Don't be rude, Emma.
Emma:	Sorry.
Linda:	To Richard.
Emma:	Sorry.
Richard:	Not at all. I always forget that not everyone's interested in that sort of thing.
Linda:	That's all right, love. Emma's just tired. We should leave you alone, shouldn't we? We've interrupted your work.
Richard:	Yes, sorry Em.
Emma:	Emma.
Richard:	Emma, yes, sorry Emma. Well, I'll see you later maybe. Bring a friend if you like.
Emma:	Bye.

[Linda exits. Richard follows but stops just as he gets to the door.]

Richard:	You know, Emma, I'm really not . . .

[Pause]

Emma: What?
Richard: Never mind. See you later.

[Richard exits. Emma sighs and picks up her book.
After a few seconds she throws it down.]

Emma: Somebody help me. What's the point?
                   What is the point?

[Emma turns the TV on with a remote control. When
Saltmine performed this we indicated the TV by shining
a light up at Emma's face and playing a recorded voice
for the Newsreaders. We hear:]

Newsreader   The comet will be seen most clearly
1:   in —

[Emma changes the channel with the remote.]

Newsreader   Having travelled for tens of millions of
2:   miles, the comet won't be seen again
                   for –

[Emma changes the channel with the remote again.]

Newsreader   The census should give us the most
3:   detailed picture yet of the people of
                   Britain. Now back to our main story:
                   the skies will be illuminated tonight
                   by . . .

[Emma turns the TV to a dead channel and lets her head
slump onto the table. There is silence. Then, unseen by
Emma, the TV flickers into life again.]

Newsreader   The comet has . . . it's stopped. It's
4:   come to rest over a small town . . .
                            over a stable . . .

[The stage goes dark but for the light of the TV. The
company sings the 'Coventry Carol'. As the lights
come up they reveal the company frozen in a series
of tableaux depicting the nativity. The first one shows
Joseph helping Mary to walk to Bethlehem. The lights go
down and the company change position. As they come
up again we see Mary placing Jesus in the manger. The
final tableau shows the adoration of Jesus by the Magi.
Emma lifts her head and sees the final image. She gets
up from her chair and walks over so that she briefly
becomes a part of it, then she stands and watches the
next scene unfold. As the lights dim on the final image
the carol dies away and instead we hear the company
creating birdsong and the sounds of a river. The lights
come up and the scene has been transformed into the
river Jordan. This has been created very simply with a
blue cloth rippled by the company members. John the
Baptist stands in the middle of the river, in a hole slit
in the cloth.]

John: Mine is the voice of one crying in the
                            desert, 'Prepare the way for the Lord!'

[The crowd, played by the actors rippling the 'river',
murmur amongst themselves 'He's mad!' 'No, he's a
prophet!' 'He's the messiah' and so on.]

John: No, I am not God's Holy One. I baptize
                            with water but he will baptize with
                            the Holy Spirit and with fire.

[The crowd responds again. Suddenly, the actor playing Jesus stands up and approaches John.]

John: Behold, the Lamb of God who takes
                   away the sins of the world.

[They embrace as the crowd reacts.]

Jesus: Would you baptize me, John?

[John laughs before realizing that Jesus is serious.]

John: No, no. Surely you should baptize me?
Jesus: Please, it needs to be this way.

[There is a pause as John considers this, and then without another word he baptizes Jesus in the river. The whole company say God's line:]

Voice: This is my son who I love. I delight in
                   him!

[The lights go down.]

Scene Two

[We hear the static of the TV again, and when the lights come up Emma is alone on stage.]

Emma: What a strange dream. I've been
                   working too hard.

[She turns the TV off, picks up the Bible and flicks through it.]

Emma:	Then the Spirit led Jesus into the desert to be tempted by the devil.
Linda:	[off] Emma! Richard is going.
Emma:	[to herself] Good.

[Enter Linda and Richard.]

Linda:	Well, goodbye love. I'll see you soon.

[Richard and Linda embrace.]

Richard:	See you later. Bye, Em.
Emma:	Emma.

[Richard exits.]

Linda:	Are you all right, Emma?
Emma:	Yeah, fine, I just fell asleep and had a funny dream.
Linda:	You work too hard, that's your trouble.
Emma:	Is it? Is that 'my trouble'?
Linda:	What are you studying now anyway?
Emma:	You mean you don't know?
Linda:	I'm sorry love, it's just I've been busy.
Emma:	With Richard?
Linda:	At work! And by the way, I won't have you being rude to him. I know you've been working hard but that's no excuse. He's a lovely man who really cares about us.
Emma:	About you.
Linda:	About you too if you'd only let him.
Emma:	He's not my Dad.
Linda:	He's not trying to be, Emma, he's really not. Emma, I know the last two years

	have been – don't you think I miss him too? Come on, let's not fight. What work are you doing?
Emma:	R.E.; the life of Christ.
Linda:	Oh, interesting.
Emma:	Well, sort of. No one else at school really cares about it.
Linda:	Do you?
Emma:	I just want to do well.
Linda:	Well, I always loved those stories. Are they true, do you think?
Emma:	The stories? We don't really do that, Mum. We look at whether they've been changed and how they've been edited, you know this.
Linda:	Yes, but I never understand why it matters if it's not true?
Emma:	Because people believe they're true and because they've had such an impact that . . . I don't know, it just matters.
Linda:	I see. Cup of tea?
Emma:	Please.

[Linda exits. Emma smiles to herself and picks up her book again.]

Emma: Then Jesus was led by the Spirit into the desert to be tempted by the devil.

[Behind Emma, Jesus staggers on.]

Emma: Mum?
Linda: [off] Coming, love.

[Linda enters, puts a cup of tea on the table, and then exits. Emma turns around and sees Jesus. He is in a seriously bad way, tangled hair, matted beard and so on.]

Emma: W–what are you . . . ? What are you
                 doing here?
Jesus: I'm hungry.

[Instantly he is distracted by something. We hear the whispering of Satan but we see nothing.]

Satan: If you are God's Son, order these stones
                 to be turned into bread. If you are
                 God's Son, order these stones to be
                 turned into bread.
Jesus: Man does not only live by bread, but
                 on every word that comes from the
                 mouth of God.

[From somewhere else Jesus hears Satan's voice again. We hear the whispers.]

Satan: If you are God's Son, throw yourself
                 down. God will send his angels to
                 protect you. If you are God's Son –
Emma: Who are you speaking to?
Jesus: To him. It is also written: do not put
                 the Lord your God to the test!
Emma: I can't see anyone!
Jesus: Wait.

[A dark figure appears behind them. He wears a black hooded robe and a white neutral mask. He leans on a thick gnarled wooden staff.]

Satan: I will give you everything, if you will bow down and worship me.

[He sweeps his hand before Jesus and the two of them are suddenly bathed in golden light.]

Jesus: Get away from me, Satan! It is written: worship the Lord your God and serve only him.

Satan: As you wish.

[Satan goes to strike Jesus with his staff. It would be a killing blow but the staff stops just inches from Jesus' head. Satan fights hard to push through the invisible barrier that seems to stop him, but he cannot. He puts the staff down and repeats:]

Satan: As you wish.

[Satan exits.]

Emma: Here, drink this.

[She gives Jesus her tea, which he gratefully drinks.]

Jesus: Thank you.

Emma: Are you all right?

Jesus: I'm fine. At least, I will be.

[Jesus finishes the tea and hands the mug back to her. He starts to exit.]

Emma: Where are you going?

Jesus: Not far. I need to start my work. Emma –

Emma: You know my name?
Jesus: Yes. You can follow if you like.

[Jesus exits, leaving Emma holding the mug. Linda enters and sees the empty mug in Emma's hand.]

Linda: Gosh, you drank that quickly! A little
                          thirsty were we, love?
Emma: Um, yes.
Linda: Well, let me take your mug.

[Linda takes the mug from Emma and exits with it. Emma is left anxiously on stage.]

Emma: Hello? Hello?

[Shaken, Emma sits down. She looks at the Bible and begins to read. Then she nervously puts it down again. Linda enters again.]

Linda: Did you say something?
Emma: Yes. No.
Linda: Well, that gives me a choice.
Emma: It's not important.
Linda: All right then. Now, about this party
                          . . .
Emma: Um . . .
Linda: You know it would mean a lot to
                          Richard if you came, and to me.
Emma: Right.
Linda: And I do think it would do you good
                          to get out of the house for a while.
Emma: Yes.
Linda: Yes, it would do you good, or yes,
                          you'll come?

Emma:	Yes.
Linda:	Emma!
Emma:	What? Oh, sorry, yes, yes I'll come.
Linda:	Honestly, I bet you're still thinking about your work aren't you?
Emma:	Um, yes.
Linda:	Come on, it looks like you need that party more than I thought!

Scene Three

[We hear the sounds of the party – laughter and so on. Emma, Richard and Jesus enter. Jesus stands upstage. Emma and Richard talk downstage.]

Richard:	I'm sorry it's so cloudy, Emma.
Emma:	It's all right. We'll see the comet next time.
Richard:	I think that'll be in about a million years.
Emma:	Oh, did you have plans then?
Richard:	No, no, I think I'm free. I mean, I was going to decompose that day but I guess I can reschedule.
Emma:	Perfect.
Richard:	So how's the work going?
Emma:	Oh, all right. I think I needed a break from it though.
Richard:	Boring?
Emma:	No, no, I don't think I could call it boring. I think maybe I just needed a break from it.
Richard:	I know what you mean. I constantly need a break from my work.

	Anything to distract me from that! Hence the interest in comets, probably.
Emma:	Do you believe any of it, Richard?
Richard:	What, comets? Oh, you mean your work? The Bible?
Emma:	Yes.
Richard:	You know, I sort of think I do. What about you?
Emma:	I'm . . . I'm not sure. Seems too far-fetched.
Richard:	Oh, lots of things in my life are far-fetched. I sometimes feel my life is a film. I'm just watching it happen.
Emma:	How's the plot?
Richard:	Of the film? Pretty far-fetched, and you know, I sometimes get the feeling I've seen it before. How's yours?
Emma:	Plot?
Richard:	Life.
Emma:	I don't know. I'm not really thinking about it. I'm just trying to pass my exam.
Richard:	Are you? Well, to answer your question: yes, I've always sort of believed. I think if this is all there is to this movie then I definitely want my money back, although knowing me I won't quite have the courage to ask for it. I'll probably just settle for being a bit grumpy with the usherettes. Anyway, I'd better go and mingle. Look, Emma, thanks for coming. I really appreciate it.
Emma:	Thank you for having me.

[Richard retreats to mingle with the other guests. As he does, Jesus steps forward from the back of the party. He looks a lot healthier than when we last saw him.]

Jesus:	That was nice.
Emma:	What on earth are you doing here?
Jesus:	I'm one of the guests. Anyway, I'm glad you made friends with Richard. I've always liked him.
Emma:	Have you? You've always liked him. Hmm, must be his winning personality, I expect. I must be going mad.
Jesus:	You aren't insane.
Emma:	Oh, I'm not insane! Excellent! So everyone else here can see you, can they?
Jesus:	Well, actually, no.
Emma:	'Well, actually, no.' So I'm having a conversation with my invisible friend at a party, but don't worry, he says I'm not insane. 'Who says that, Emma?' Well, funny you should ask that, man-in-white coat: Jesus says that. Yes, Jesus tells me that I am not insane! I suppose you like me as well. Perhaps you find me charmingly eccentric.
Jesus:	I just thought you might like to see the next bit of the story.
Emma:	The next bit?
Jesus:	Yes, you seemed to be having trouble picturing it, but I'll go if you want.
Emma:	What are you talking about? Yes, I want you to go, you're ruining my life!

[Just then we hear Richard saying 'What, it's all gone? But I thought I had loads more wine in the cellar!' The sounds of the party slowly turn to disgruntlement. Richard and Linda are being criticized on either side of the stage. We see them defending themselves and backing away from their critics. They end up back to back, miming increasingly frantic explanations.]

Emma: You have got to be kidding me.

Jesus: So, do you want me to go?

[There is a pause as Emma thinks about what is about to happen.]

Emma: Stay exactly where you are.

[Linda approaches from the back, looking a little upset. Again, she doesn't see Jesus.]

Linda: Honestly, this is ever so embarrassing. He's totally run out of wine, I can't understand it. I thought we'd bought more than enough. Everyone will be drinking water at this rate.

[Emma exchanges a look with Jesus.]

Emma: Mum, would you mind getting me a glass of water?

Linda: Of course, love. There you are.

[She pours Emma a glass of water. It turns into wine. Saltmine did this through the use of food colouring in the bottom of the glass. Linda doesn't notice.]

Emma: Thanks.

[Linda goes upstage to join Richard.]

Richard: Ah, you found some wine, excellent! I
                thought you might.

[Richard and Linda exit. Emma drinks the wine
appreciatively.]

Emma: All right. That was good. You can stay.
Jesus: Thanks.
Emma: And was it really like that?
Jesus: What, back then?

[Emma nods.]

Jesus: More or less. Do you want to see the
                rest?
Emma: Of the story?
Jesus: Yes.
Emma: Will it help me with my R.E.?
Jesus: Only if you can decide if I'm editing it
                or not.
Emma: Is that a joke?
Jesus: Sort of.
Emma: You're not really supposed to tell jokes,
                you know.
Jesus: Sorry. So, do you want to see?
Emma: Yes.
Jesus: It's not all nice, you know.
Emma: I'd like to see.

[Blackout.]

Scene Four

[The company sings. As the lights come up we see a cripple, Abel, sitting on the stage. The lighting suggests that there is water in front of him. Emma enters and approaches him.]

Emma:	Excuse me. Can you tell me where I am?
Abel:	You, my dearest, are at the pool of Bethesda.
Emma:	Have you been here long?
Abel:	In total?
Emma:	Yes.
Abel:	Thirty-seven, no, no, I tell a lie, thirty-eight years.
Emma:	Really?!
Abel:	It's the honest blasted truth with no word of a lie.
Emma:	Gosh!
Abel:	And not a day less. Not a day.
Emma:	Thirty-eight years!
Abel:	Most of my life.
Emma:	Well, why have you been here so long?
Abel:	Dear God! Isn't it obvious? Look at me! I'm crippled, aren't I? I'm crippled. I'm here to be healed. But you only get healed when an angel disturbs the water, and any fool knows the angels only disturb the water from time to time, though God knows why. And what's more, only the first person into the water gets healed anyway so I'm out of luck; half the cripples here have all their mates just

waiting to push the rest of us back. I
was nearly in last time. I could
nearly touch this shining golden
water but this miserable whole-bodied
swine got me by the collar and . . .
they pushed me back. They always
do.

[Jesus walks up behind them.]

Emma: Well, where are all your friends and
              family?
Abel: What friends? What family? I'm on my
              own, aren't I? Nobody cares about me
              – a blasted old scoundrel who got
              what was coming to him.
              They're right as well: that's me.
              Anyway, what do you care? What are
              you, a tourist?
Emma: No I'm just –
Abel: Well clear off!
Emma: I'm sorry.
Abel: Get lost.
Jesus: Do you want to get well?

[Abel turns on Jesus.]

Abel: I swear if you weren't so tall I'd throttle
              you! Of course I want to get well! But
              no one will help me, will they? No
              one will help me. They just stand
              there making damn fool remarks!
              Well, damn you, get lost!
Jesus: Get up, pick up your mat and walk.

Abel: How dare you? How dare you? Making
                   fun of an old ma–

[Abel stops as he feels something in his legs. Slowly,
and with something like awe, he stretches his legs and
gets to his feet.]

Abel: Well, I'll be. I've never . . . that is to say
                   I've never . . . I can walk. I can walk!

[He begins to bounce and jump and caper.]

Abel: I can walk! I can jump! I can walk!
                   I can walk, I can jump, I can walk!

[He grabs Emma and spins her round. Abruptly he
stops and comes to stand in front of Jesus.]

Abel: Thank you sir! Thank you!

[There is a simultaneous explosion of talking from the
company 'Healing on the Sabbath!' 'Just imagine!' 'It's
a scandal!' 'It's not right!' 'Well, he healed me!' It turns
into a little verse or song:]

Company: Healing on the Sabbath! (No!)
                   Healing on the Sabbath!
                   He was lying flat,
                   Now he's got his mat,
                   I've never seen anyone dance like that!
                   Healing on the Sabbath (Shame!)
                   Healing on the Sabbath!
                   It's against the law,
                   But you must adore

The man who raised him from the floor,
The man who raised him from the floor!

[As that finishes the company gathers to form the crowd to which Jesus speaks. They react boisterously, laughing and applauding when they hear something they like.]

Jesus: Blessed are the poor in spirit, for theirs is the kingdom of heaven. Blessed are those who mourn, for they shall be comforted. Come to me all who are weak and weighed down with life's troubles and I shall give you rest. But don't think that I have come to abolish the law or the prophets; I haven't, I've come to fulfil them. And I say that unless your righteousness is greater than that of the teachers of the law, you will not enter the kingdom of heaven.

[There is laughter at the apparent absurdity of this.]

Jesus: I know you've heard it said 'An eye for an eye and a tooth for a tooth', but I say if someone hits you on your right cheek, turn the other cheek to him as well. If someone wants to sue you and take the shirt from your back, give him your coat into the bargain. If someone forces you to go one mile, go with him two miles. Give freely to anyone who asks

you and don't reject someone who
wants to borrow from you. You
have heard that it was said 'Love
your neighbour and hate your
enemy', but I say love your enemies
and bless those who curse you, do
good to the people that hate you and
pray for those who hurt you.

[Pause as Jesus surveys the crowd. They are listening
very closely now.]

Jesus:　　　　Do not judge or you will be judged
too. For in the same way as you
judge and with the measure you use,
so it will be applied to you. Why do
you look at the little speck of
sawdust in your brother's eye when
there is a great plank of wood in
your own eye? Don't be hypocritical.
First deal with the plank in your own
eye, then maybe you will see clearly
to remove the speck in your brother's
eye.

Scene Five

[The company sings and the Pharisee actors put on
their masks.]

Pharisee 1:　　The point is he was carrying his mat
on the Sabbath; this constitutes work
and is against the law. This miracle-
worker causes people to break the
law of our fathers.

Pharisee 2: The point is he said that God is his father.

Pharisee 1: The point is he is a blasphemer and must be silenced.

Pharisee 3: If you will allow me. I am the eldest here; my life has been devoted to serving God and to keeping his law. This Jesus has great power, yes? The people love him, yes? Even while we talk here, the crowds gather. Soon it will be too late for us to do anything. But the devil himself has great power and the people will no longer love him if he speaks blasphemy.

Pharisee 1: But what if he really is the messiah?

Pharisee 3: If he is the messiah, why has he not come to us? Why does he spend his time with tax collectors, with sinners, with people who do not obey the law? Why does he encourage his disciples to break the Sabbath laws?

Pharisee 2: If he were the messiah, would we not have known it before now? Have we not been waiting for this day, scouring the Scripture for clues as to when the messiah would come?

Pharisee 3: Invite this prophet to your house, we shall see this wisdom that we have heard spoken of, we will trap him with our questions until he cannot help but blaspheme. Then we will

have him killed. The people are fickle;
they will believe whatever we tell
them to believe. The same people that
now acclaim him to the echo will
soon bay for his blood.

Pharisee 1:   Pray God it will not come to that!

Pharisee 3:   These are desperate times, brother. Who
knows what measures we may have
to employ?

[The scene changes to a meal. The company sings a
slow melancholy song. Emma and Jesus enter. Pharisee
2 indicates where they should sit. As the song continues
the Pharisee turns to the audience and Emma turns to
Jesus.]

Emma: Why have we come here?

Jesus: Wait a moment.

[A woman, Mary Magdalene, enters. She is crying and
carrying a bottle of perfume. She wets Jesus' feet and
dries them with her hair. She speaks to herself as much
as to the audience.]

Mary: All I ever wanted . . . all I ever needed
. . . and here I was with nothing.
Nothing I could offer. Nothing but
shame and the metallic taste of my
sin. His fame had spread throughout
the country. Everyone had heard of
him, his fame had spread like fire or
the lies that men tell. And then came
the news that he was coming to our
town. A new kind of rabbi, a man
who taught of love, who spoke to

	everyone: to children, to foreigners, to women, even to . . .
Pharisee 2:	That's Mary the prostitute. Watch.
Mary:	So I took the money, all the money and I spent it on this perfume. I spent it knowing that he would reject me and that the nothingness I'd had before would consume me. I spent the money, I bought the perfume and I took it with my shame to him. All I ever wanted . . . all I ever needed . . .

[Mary anoints Jesus' feet.]

Pharisee 2:	What kind of a prophet allows a woman like that to touch him? He's failing the test!

[As Jesus tells his story he divides his attention between Mary and the Pharisee.]

Jesus:	My friends, let me tell you a story. Two men owed money to a moneylender: one owed fifty pounds and the other five hundred, but neither could pay. The moneylender cancelled the debt of both men. Now, which man loved him most?
Pharisee 2:	The one that had owed the most money.
Jesus:	I think you are right. Now, I have been invited to your house but you gave me no water for my feet. This woman has washed my feet with her own tears. You gave me no oil for my head; this woman has anointed my

feet with perfume. I say her many
sins are forgiven because she has
loved much. The person who is
forgiven little, loves little.

[To Mary.]

Jesus: Your sins are forgiven; your faith has
saved you. Go in peace.

[Mary cannot quite believe what she has heard, and
slowly stands and looks at Jesus. Gradually she
understands and smiles. She exits. There is silence for
a moment before the barely suppressed explosion from
the Pharisee.]

Pharisee 2:   Who is this man who says he can
forgive sins? Only God can do that!
He's trapped himself.

Emma: Let's go.

[As Jesus speaks he seems to be a different character
than we have seen before, as though the divine part of
his nature is being glimpsed. As Jesus begins to speak,
Pharisee 2 cowers away.]

Jesus: My Father is always at work and I too
am working. The son can do nothing
by himself but only what he sees the
father doing. You will be amazed, but
you will see greater things than these,
for just as the father gives life so shall
the son give life to whom he is
pleased to give it. The father judges
no one but has entrusted judgement

	to his son. I'm telling you the truth: whoever hears my word and believes will have eternal life.
Pharisee 2:	Blasphemy!
Emma:	Please, let's just go.
Jesus:	You study the Scriptures diligently; you pore over them day and night, because you think that by them you possess eternal life. But these are Scriptures that testify and prophesy about me, yet you refuse to come to me to have that life! I know you, I know your hearts. You do not have the love of God. How can you, when you accept the flattering praises of each other but neglect to win the praises that come from the only God? But don't think that I will accuse you before my Father. I will not. Your accuser will be Moses, the one who received the law on which your hopes are set. If you believed Moses then you would believe me, for he wrote about me. But since you do not believe what he wrote, how are you going to believe what I say?

[As the speech progresses Pharisee 2 gets smaller and smaller until he is a crumpled ball at Jesus' feet. Lights down. The company remain at the back of the stage.]

Scene Six

Emma: You shouldn't do that. You shouldn't antagonize them like that.

Jesus: Don't be afraid, Emma.

Emma: I'm not afraid for me, I'm afraid for you. I know how this story ends.

Jesus: If you know how it ends, why are you afraid?

Emma: Because you die.

Jesus: Not for long. Comparatively speaking.

Emma: Be serious, I don't . . .

Jesus: What?

Emma: I don't believe that.

Jesus: You don't believe . . .

Emma: In the resurrection. I don't believe you can come back. I want to but I just can't. And since I'm imagining this story, this time you won't come back. I know you won't. People die and they don't come back. They don't come back however much you want them to. So don't upset them. I know you believe what you're saying, but just stay out of their way!

Jesus: I have to do what my father wants.

Emma: What about what you want?

Jesus: Emma, please don't tempt me. I might not like everything I have to do but I want to do my father's will. Don't be scared. I will help you believe, just like I've helped you imagine.

Emma: You can't.

Jesus: Don't you trust me?

[As they finish talking the rest of the company construct the boat. This is a very simple structure, possibly using the coat-stand from the back of the stage. It is made believable by the movements and the sounds of the sea made by the company.]

Jesus: Let's go to the other side of the lake.

[As they set off, Jesus falls asleep in the back of the boat. As they journey it is clear that the weather is taking a turn for the worse and finally a full-blown storm has erupted. The lighting is dark, the sound is almost deafening and the boat is pitching dangerously, possibly the sail could collapse or tear.]

Disciple 1:   I've never seen anything like this!
Disciple 2:   Where's the master?
Emma: I think he's asleep in the back.
Disciple 1:   How can he sleep in this? Wake him up!
Disciple 2:   Master, what are you doing? What are you doing? We're going to drown!

[Jesus stands and addresses the elements.]

Jesus: Be still!

[The storm dies away.]

Jesus: Where is your faith?
Disciple 1:   Who is he? Even the elements obey him.
Emma: Oh, be quiet.

[The boat is removed. There is a babble of voices discussing different miracles as the company sit in a semicircle around Jesus.]

Teacher of the Law: Master, what must I do to have eternal life?

[Reaction from the crowd: 'Aye, that's what I'd like to know!', laughter and so on.]

Jesus: Well, you know the Scriptures. What do they tell you?

Teacher of the Law: Love the Lord your God with all your strength, heart, soul and mind and love your neighbour as yourself.

Jesus: You're right, do all this and you will be saved.

Teacher of the Law: But who is my neighbour?

[As Jesus tells the story of the Good Samaritan the rest of the company act it out. There's no reason why, instead of Jesus telling the whole thing himself, the characters couldn't narrate their parts of the story: the man, the priest and so on. Possibly the audience could also help tell the story.]

Jesus: Once there was a man who went on a journey from Jerusalem to Jericho when he fell into the hands of robbers. They beat him and they stripped him and then they went on their way leaving him half dead. A priest was walking by on the other side of the road, saw the man and quickly hurried on. Then a man of the law came along, but when he saw the man he too rushed by on the other side of the road. Finally, a Samaritan walked by and when he saw the man he felt pity for him. He bandaged his wounds, put him on his donkey and took him to a nearby inn. He paid the innkeeper and told him to look after the injured man until he returned, when he would reimburse the innkeeper for any expense. Now, which man out of the three do you think was the good neighbour to the injured man?

Teacher of the Law: The one who had mercy on him.

Jesus: So go and do the same.

Emma: Can I ask a question?

Jesus: Of course.

Emma: Why do you let everyone ask you questions and interrupt? Why don't you just preach like they do in church?

Jesus: Because people want to ask me things specific to them. Everyone is different, everyone wants to know something different, so sometimes I tell them things that are true for everyone and sometimes I tell individuals what they need to know.

Scene Seven

[Mary, sister of Martha, enters.]

Mary: My Lord!

[Mary kneels at Jesus' feet.]

Jesus: What is it, Mary? I'm glad to see you!

Mary: My Lord, my brother who I know you love, he's sick. Martha and I are so frightened. Please come quickly. I know you can make him well.

Jesus: I know your brother. He is my friend. Don't be frightened, Mary, this illness of his will not end in death.

Mary: Then please come quickly! If he is your friend, Jesus, please come.

Jesus: Let's go to our friend.

Emma: But surely if the illness won't end in death then there is no need for us to go? Jesus, the Pharisees will be around. It isn't safe.

Jesus: He is dead, Emma.

Emma: But you said he wouldn't die!

Jesus: I said what I said. And for your sake I'm glad that I wasn't there to save him although he is my friend. But still we have to go to him.

[As Emma and Jesus talk, the mourners gather behind them dressed in black. We hear the sounds of the mourning begin. As Jesus and Emma reach the group Mary turns on them, really upset.]

Mary: Didn't I say he was sick? Why did you wait? Master, I trusted you! I trusted you!

Jesus: Carry on trusting me, Mary.

Mary: How can I? If you had been here I know he wouldn't have died.

Jesus: He will rise again.

Mary: Perhaps. Perhaps as we all will in the resurrection at the end of time.

Jesus: Listen to me, all of you: I am the resurrection and the life. The person who believes in me will not die but have eternal life. Do you believe this? Do you?

Mary: I believe that you are the Christ, the Son of the living God.

Jesus: Take the stone away from the tomb.

Emma: But he's been dead for four days!

Mary: Please do what he tells you.

[Emma and Mary slowly open the wardrobe. Lazarus falls out, quite dead. Everyone stares in shock at the half-naked corpse on the floor. Suddenly Lazarus inhales deeply and begins to move. Mary rushes to her brother's side. He looks up, sees Jesus, smiles and starts to laugh.]

Lazarus: Well, it's nice to see you again, my friend. I'm sorry I'm not properly dressed.

Jesus: How's your faith, Emma?

[Lazarus and Jesus hug. Emma is left isolated, shaking her head in disbelief.]

[Blackout. The company become the money-changers and traders at the temple. They use the books from Emma's desk to create a flock of pigeons that circle the stage around Emma and Jesus. Then they go into different sales patter as they harangue the audience, offering to change money or sell pigeons for sacrifice. The actors playing Emma and Jesus are thrown flat caps by the other company members and briefly become street traders; they bombard the audience with sales pitches. With a shout Jesus tears the hat from his head and hurls it to the back of the stage. At that moment the rest of the company freeze in position, in mid sentence. Silence.]

Emma: Where are we?

Jesus: The temple in Jerusalem.

Emma: Why have we come here? We should
                   stay away from here! This is where
                             . . .

[But Jesus is only half-listening. Dead slow, he walks towards one of the traders. With one hand he picks him up by the throat.]

Jesus: It is written 'My house will be called a
                   house of prayer', but you have turned
                   it into a den of thieves!

[He hurls the trader away. The spell is broken and an angry roar erupts. The traders mime gathering as many of their scattered possessions as they can, grabbing knives and so on, and gather round Jesus like jackals around a lion.]

Traders: How dare you?

Jesus: How dare I? This is my father's house!

Traders: We have the permission of the High Priest!

Jesus: Then tell the High Priest this: the tax collectors and the prostitutes are entering the kingdom of God ahead of you!

[Blasted by his anger, the traders flee. Jesus and Emma exit. The company move quickly, putting on their masks and becoming Pharisees.]

Scene Eight

Pharisee 3: He cannot live.

Pharisee 1: And cannot die. Not while the crowd still loves him.

Pharisee 2: He caused disturbance in the holy temple, he has openly defied us.

Pharisee 3: We are the guardians of God's law on earth. We have a responsibility. If the people see a man with no respect for us then they see the law disrespected. If they lose respect for the law then they will lose respect for God.

Pharisee 1: I have not seen him disrespect God. I have only seen him disrespect us. Let us be careful that we do what we do for the right reasons.

Pharisee 2: Really, why are we arguing about this? The man has claimed he is the Son of God. He has to be removed, that is clear. But how to do it? As my friend

has said, and I say again, the crowd
loves him.

Pharisee 3:   You have too much faith in the people,
my friend. They love him because
he mocks authority, and because he
pretends to care for them. But does
he care? Where will this end? Hmm?
Sooner or later the Romans will hear
about this messiah and the whole
weight of their war machine will
come crashing down on one small,
poorly defended city called Jerusalem.
Will one man be enough to defend
us? No. Will they love him when
their city is in flames? No, they
will curse him, they will hate him
and they will wish that someone had
the courage to do what we are doing
now.

Pharisee 2:   But how to do it? He is popular and
we know that his disciples will not
stand idly by while we seize him. If
we involve the soldiers we could have
a full-scale riot on our hands. Are you
prepared for that?

Pharisee 3:   No, indeed I am not. That is why one
of his own must give him up
without fuss. Someone he would not
suspect.

Pharisee 1:   And do you know of such a person?

Pharisee 3:   I do. They are here now. Why don't
you show them in, my friend?

[Pharisee 1 goes to the side of the stage and brings
Emma in with him.]

Pharisee 3: Now, my dear, are you willing to do what you say you will do?

Emma: He isn't to be harmed. Do you understand? Lock him up, do what you want, but don't hurt him.

Pharisee 3: Of course.

Emma: I have your word?

Pharisee 3: I said of course.

Emma: Fine. I'll hug him. That will be your signal.

Pharisee 2: You know I would feel a lot happier about this if you would accept some small payment, as a token of our appreciation. In many ways you are saving our city.

Emma: Listen to me; I'm not doing this for you. You mean nothing to me. But I know that if I don't give him up someone else will and they won't care if you kill him. So you can keep your money, so long as I have your word.

[Emma exits.]

Pharisee 1: I wash my hands of this.

[Blackout.]

Scene Nine

[The lights come up but stay low. Jesus is praying.]

Jesus: Father, Father if it is possible let this
                    responsibility be taken from me. But
                    let your will be done, not mine,
                    Father. Always, Father: your will, not
                    mine.

[Emma enters. Jesus looks at her. They hold eye contact
for a moment.]

Jesus: Amen.
Emma: Look . . .
Jesus: Do what you're going to do quickly,
                    Emma.
Emma: I'm sorry. It was the only way.
Jesus: Yes, it was the only way.

[The company sing the 'Coventry Carol' as in the
nativity section, and form a series of tableaux depicting
Jesus' trial and execution. The first shows Jesus before
Pilate. The second is Jesus being scourged. The final
tableau shows Jesus on the cross. Emma stands, crying,
at the foot of the cross.]

Emma: I'm sorry. They said you would be
                    spared. They promised. I told you
                    this would happen. Why didn't you
                    listen to me? I told you.

[There is a long silence. We hear laughter, quietly at
first, but growing louder and louder. Then we hear
the sound of someone walking closer. Satan enters, his

staff hitting the ground as he walks. He approaches the crucified Jesus and laughs in his face. Then he exits and we go to blackout. When the lights come up the set is back to how it was at the start of the play. Emma is slumped at her desk. She lifts her head. Pause. Enter Linda.]

Linda: Hello love, I might have known I'd find you here. I'll tell you one thing, I'm not as young as I was. I used to be able to stay out with my friends all night and still have energy the next day! But nowadays, well the party's in full swing and I've had to come away early. Not as early as you, of course, you workaholic! Have you been crying?

Emma: I've had a horrible dream, Mum. I dreamed that I betrayed Jesus and he died because of me.

[Linda laughs at first but as soon as she sees that Emma's really upset she puts her arm around her daughter.]

Linda: Oh dear! You're overtired love, that's all.

Emma: I know, but it was a horrible dream.

Linda: Just a dream. I sometimes dream that I go to work and when I get there I realize that I'm not wearing any clothes, but I haven't actually done that for ages. Honestly love, you know when you dwell on things like you've been doing, working non-stop, and reading every hour that God sends, it can prey on your mind. That's all that's happened.

Emma: Maybe. I don't think so. I feel awful.
Linda: Maybe you drank too much at the
                    party. I think what you need is a nice
                    cup of tea!

[As Linda leaves she calls over her shoulder to
Emma.]

Linda: Tea is a panacea you know! Richard
                    taught me that word the other day. It
                    means it cures everything!

[Linda exits. There is another blackout. In the darkness
we hear voices saying 'Come closer, come closer, we
have news!' The company goes into the audience with
torches or lanterns and each company member stands
in a different section. Then the male actors deliver the
first speech and the females give the second.)

Speech 1:   Come closer, there's news. He's been
                    seen. I'm telling you he's been seen.
                    It was like this, after his death we
                    were scared, dead scared. We
                    gathered together and we prayed.
                    We prayed and we didn't go out. See,
                    we knew that once they'd got rid
                    of the Master they wouldn't think
                    twice about stamping us out, about
                    swatting us like flies. Anyway, I was
                    there in this room with the others
                    when there's this knock on the door
                    – we froze. Sweat dribbled down our
                    faces. I was all for going out the back
                    way but then we hear Mary's voice
                    calling us from the other side of the

door. Of course we open up and
pull her inside. I was furious. 'Are
you mad? What are you doing?' I
said. 'Don't you understand? You
were seen! You were seen with him!
You can't go out, it's not safe!' But
there was something in her eyes that
stopped me dead. 'The stone's been
moved,' she said. 'Jesus has risen.' I
didn't believe her at first. But over the
next few days other reports came
in. He's back, I'm telling you, he's
back! Now I've got to go, there are
other people to tell. Spread the news.

Speech 2: Listen! Come closer! There's news! I
went to the tomb. I went to his tomb
with some of the other women. We
wanted to anoint his body, you see.
To honour him. I was streaming with
tears. Then we got to the tomb and
something was wrong, terribly wrong.
The stone was rolled away; there
were no soldiers anywhere, there
was nothing. Then we saw something.
Two men – they just appeared out of
the morning sun, out of the light.
Like they were made of it. They were
dressed in white robes and we
couldn't look at their faces: like the
sun, like lightning, the tears in our
eyes made us blind with light.
Suddenly we were all afraid and
we didn't know why. So frightened.
We shook with fear; we fell,
powerless, to the ground. Then they

spoke. 'Why are you looking for the living among the dead?' We stayed silent. They said, 'He isn't here. He is risen.' Before I knew it they were gone and we were left shaking. I don't remember how, but we found ourselves stumbling back to Jerusalem. We knew we had to spread the news. He is risen. He is risen, tell everyone!

[As the whispered speeches die away so the company disperse.]

Scene Ten

[Emma returns to the stage, sitting back down at her desk. The doorbell rings and we hear Richard shouting 'Hello!' Richard enters.]

Richard:	Hi, Emma. Sorry, is your mum around?
Emma:	She's in the kitchen, making a panacea.
Richard:	Sorry?
Emma:	Tea.
Richard:	She told you!

[Emma nods. The doorbell rings.]

Richard: I'll get it.

[Richard walks across the stage and off, then back in. Mary Magdalene walks in just behind Richard. He cannot see her.]

Richard: No one was there, how odd.

[Emma doesn't look up at first.]

Emma: Must have been prank –

[She sees Mary.]

Emma: – callers.
Richard: Must have been, I suppose. I'll go and find your mum.

[Richard exits again to find Linda.]

Mary: I've seen him.
Emma: Stop it.
Mary: I've seen him.
Emma: Who?
Mary: Who? Emma, I've seen Jesus.
Emma: You're lying.
Mary: I'm not lying.
Emma: You're hysterical!
Mary: Calm down, Emma. Listen to me. I'm not lying, I'm not hysterical and I'm not alone. Other people have seen him. He sent me to tell the disciples and he particularly asked me to tell you. Look, I understand it's hard to believe. No one else believed me at first either, but now they all do.
Emma: Why?
Mary: I suppose because they've seen him too. Your tea's getting cold.

[Emma sits down and drinks some of her tea. There is a pause before she puts the tea down and looks up.]

Emma: Mary, I betrayed him. I was the one. I betrayed him.

Mary: I know that, Emma.

Emma: Even if he is alive. I looked him in the eyes and I betrayed the Son of God. Who'd want to speak with me?

Mary: Emma, look who you're talking to. If he can forgive me . . .

Emma: You didn't get him killed

Mary: I think . . . I think we all did. That's why he died. Don't you see? It was a sacrifice for us. We're all guilty, Emma. Knowing that you are is good.

Emma: It's not the same, Mary. Look, I appreciate the effort, I appreciate what you're trying to do, but it isn't the same. I'm Judas.

Mary: He was different, Emma. Trust me, his motives were different.

Emma: If he is alive, he hates me. I hate me.

[Jesus enters from behind Emma. He stands behind her and nods to Mary.]

Mary: I don't think he hates you. But maybe I'll leave you to it.

[Emma rises and crosses to Mary.]

Emma: Thank you for coming. I'm sorry I was so rude.

| Mary: | You're just in pain. I don't blame you at all. |

[There is a pause, as Emma looks at Mary. It looks as though Mary wants to say something more. Eventually she smiles and leaves. Emma turns around and sees Jesus.]

| Jesus: | Hello. |
| Emma: | Hello. |

[There is a slightly awkward pause.]

Emma:	Are you . . . OK?
Jesus:	As you see. I'm alive.
Emma:	Yes, I see that. How did that happen?
Jesus:	Me being alive?
Emma:	Yes.
Jesus:	Miracle.
Emma:	Ah yes, of course. Like Lazarus.
Jesus:	Like that.
Emma:	But I didn't believe.
Jesus:	Yes, I know. But you were just imagining, Emma. There are some things that no amount of unbelief can change.
Emma:	I should have known.
Jesus:	Well, I thought so.
Emma:	I should have believed. I'm so tired of people dying.
Jesus:	It isn't the ending you think it is.
Emma:	I'm sorry.
Jesus:	I know you are, Emma. It's all right.
Emma:	I'm so, so sorry.
Jesus:	You're forgiven.

Emma:	I'm sorry.
Jesus:	Shhhh.
Emma:	They promised me you'd be safe.
Jesus:	I'm sure they did. I said forget it. I've forgotten it.
Emma:	Did it really hurt?
Jesus:	Emma.
Emma:	Right, stupid question. Are we still friends?
Jesus:	If you want to be.
Emma:	I want to be.
Jesus:	Then we're still friends. You've got to do something for me, though.
Emma:	What?
Jesus:	You need to have faith. You've got to believe in me.
Emma:	I do.
Jesus:	And I'd like you to be nicer to your mum, she's had a hard time.
Emma:	That's not in the Bible!
Jesus:	Then just do it for me.
Emma:	All right.
Jesus:	And you can't keep all this to yourself, you know.
Emma:	I know. All right.
Jesus:	Great. Well, I'd better go. I haven't seen Peter yet and he hasn't forgiven himself either.
Emma:	OK, see you around.
Jesus:	I'm always around.
Emma:	Sure, nice for you.
Jesus:	Yes, it is.

[Jesus starts to leave.]

Emma: Wait. You still love me, don't you?

Jesus: Emma, I just died for you.

[Jesus starts to go again. Emma runs and hugs him. There is a moment where he just holds her and then she lets him go. Jesus exits.]

Linda [off]: Do you want a biscuit with your tea?

Emma: Yes please, Mum.

[Emma sits on stage. She drinks some more of her tea. She smiles. She picks up the Bible from her desk and reads aloud:]

Emma: 'As the Father has loved me, so have I loved you. Now remain in my love. If you obey my commands, you will remain in my love, just as I have obeyed my Father's commands and remain in his love. I have told you this so that my joy may be in you and that your joy may be complete. My command is this: Love each other as I have loved you. Greater love has no one than this, that he lay down his life for his friends.'

[Lights down.]